The Changing Geopolitics of Central Asia and the Caucasus

AFPC

Library of Congress Control Number: 2023913185

Paperback - 978-1-956450-78-1
Ebook - 978-1-956450-79-8

AMERICAN FOREIGN POLICY COUNCIL

AFPC Press
American Foreign Policy Council
509 C Street NE
Washington, DC 20002

in association with

ARMINLEAR

Armin Lear Press Inc
215 W Riverside Drive, #4362
Estes Park, CO 80517

The Changing Geopolitics of Central Asia and the Caucasus

Edited by

Svante E. Cornell

AFPC

Contents

Introduction

Svante E. Cornell

The geopolitical environment surrounding Central Asia and the Caucasus has changed dramatically over the past decade, with important implications for American and European interests. Regional and great powers have accorded the region ever greater attention, and the regional states themselves have developed a greater agency in responding to the geopolitical challenges confronting them. European, and in particular American, perceptions of the region have not kept up with these changes and are in need of updating.

Shifts and Shocks

The geopolitical challenges confronting the South Caucasus and Central Asia were fairly stable during the 2000s. But from 2008 onward and in an accelerating fashion, the region's challenges resulting from geopolitical competition have grown. The main reason is the virulence of Russian neo-imperialism, which manifested itself in Moscow's invasion of Georgia in August 2008. But that invasion – and its subsequent warfare in Ukraine from 2014 on – is only the tip of the iceberg: Russian pressure on all states in Central Asia and the Caucasus has increased, with Moscow ever more strongly demanding a *droit de regard* over the foreign policy of these states. Most directly, Georgia and Kazakhstan are threatened by Russian actions to destabilize their government and undermine their territorial integrity.

China's rise is in comparison both a blessing and a curse for the region. On one hand, China's interest in stability in Central Asia offers – perhaps – a modicum of deterrence to the wildest forms of Russian adventurism. But Chinese presence also threatens countries – particularly smaller ones – with unsustainable debt burdens. Central Asian states have also watched with horror as Xinjiang has been converted, essentially, to an open-air concentration camp. For Kazakhstan in particular, this poses an enormous challenge, as already strong anti-Chinese sentiment in society is supercharged by information leaking in from Western China. Meanwhile, regional governments are in no position to speak out on the matter. And in the longer term, all of Central Asia wonders what the future holds, if China displaces Russia as the dominant foreign power in the region.

In the Caucasus, Turkey and Iran are much greater players than China. Turkey played a decisive role in the 2020 Second Karabakh War, in which it effectively inserted itself as a key factor on the ground, and facilitated the Azerbaijani restoration of territorial integrity over territories occupied by Armenia since 1993. This shift of balance in turn triggered a reaction in Iran, which saw these changes as detrimental to its interests. That in turn led to a sharp deterioration of Iranian-Azerbaijani relations, with Tehran massing troops in exercises on the Azerbaijani border.

Overlayed on these more specific concerns are shocks that have changed the largely landlocked region's connections to the world. The botched U.S. withdrawal from Afghanistan dampened hopes that Central Asia would be able to develop unimpeded trade routes to the Indian Ocean to the south, the nearest connection to world seas for the region. And not long after, Russia's invasion of Ukraine led to a partial closure of the transportation routes linking China with Europe through Kazakhstan, Russia and Belarus. These events put even more pressure on the region.

Meanwhile, other powers have taken note of the growing importance of Central Asia at the center of Eurasian geopolitics. Russian and Chinese leaders visit the region frequently – Xi Jinping making Central Asia the destination of his first post-Covid foreign trip. And in recent years, heads of state or government from Turkey, India, Japan and South Korea have spent extended time period in the region as well. In parallel, links between the region and the Gulf monarchies have also developed fast.

Growing Agency

Faced with this deteriorating security situation, the states of Central Asia and the Caucasus did not sit idly by. Among them, several took action. Azerbaijan, Kazakhstan and Uzbekistan in particular took a leadership role in developing cooperative ventures to respond to the region's challenges and manage the presence and role of regional powers.

The transition of power in Uzbekistan played a critical role, with President Shavkat Mirziyoyev injecting a jolt of energy into Uzbekistan's diplomacy. He improved relations with neighbors, and in particular focused on the bilateral relationship with Kazakhstan. The two countries signed a treaty on allied relations in 2022, but this did not mean they neglected the smaller states of Central Asia. Quite to the contrary, they took measures to ensure that the smaller states bought into the concept of regional cooperation in Central Asia. Even Turkmenistan, previously largely aloof, has been a regular participant in the summits of heads of state of Central Asia.

Regional cooperation in the South Caucasus continued to be impeded by the Armenia-Azerbaijan conflict, but Azerbaijan has continued to drive trilateral cooperation with Georgia and Turkey. Meanwhile, there has been a considerable development of Trans-Caspian cooperation, with diplomatic initiatives linking Azerbaijan with Kazakhstan, Turkmenistan, and Uzbekistan expanding rapidly in frequency and scope.

Western Reaction

The Western reaction to this state of affairs has been relatively lukewarm. The EU has sought to expand its presence in the region, not least in Central Asia where it is the largest donor. The EU has upgraded the level of its interaction with Central Asian states to the presidential level, EU Council President Charles Michel traveling to Central Asia for summits with regional presidents in both 2022 and 2023. The EU has also taken a greater interest in energy supplies from the region, Commission President Ursula von der Leyen inking a Strategic Partnership in the field of energy with Azerbaijan in 2022. The EU has also gotten involved at the highest level in mediating the deadlock in Georgian politics and the Armenia-Azerbaijan conflict, with mixed results.

As for the United States, it has yet to engage meaningfully with the region in a strategic way. This is somewhat surprising, given the designation of strategic competition with China and Russia as the main focus of U.S. national security strategy. The U.S. did host two Central Asian presidents for state visits in 2018, and

Secretary of State Antony Blinken visited Central Asia in 2023, while also engaging in efforts to find a lasting solution to the Armenia-Azerbaijan conflict. But a more consistent U.S. presence that approaches the region strategically has largely been missing.

New Perspectives

This volume seeks to contribute to a greater understanding of the strategic challenges facing Central Asia and the Caucasus. In so doing, the Central Asia-Caucasus Institute has collected some of the finest minds observing the shifting geopolitics of the region. Intentionally, we have sought to provide equal attention to the shifting strategies of great powers, and of the reactions of regional states themselves. Unlike what is commonly believed in Western capitals, states in Central Asia and the Caucasus are no longer pawns on a "Grand Chessboard" or objects of a "Great Game." They are very much actors in their own right, capable – at least in the case of the stronger countries in the region – of taking matters into their own hands and contributing to shaping the future of their region.

A Steadily Tightening Embrace: China's Ascent in Central Asia and the Caucasus

Raffaello Pantucci

*Chinese engagement with Central Asia and the Caucasus
has been on a steady ascent. China accords considerably more
importance to Central Asia than to the Caucasus, and the
absolutely central aspect of Chinese engagement is Xinjiang.
The economic push into Central Asia has continued, in spite of
a slowdown in investment and trade during the pandemic.
Among outside powers, Russia is the only power that Beijing
considers a genuine wholesale competitor, and even then,
that relationship is seen through the lens of cooperation at the
larger, strategic level. This has been complicated by the invasion of Ukraine, but so far this has not particularly expressed
itself – narratives of a vacuum opening which China is filling
are vastly overplayed. China does faces challenges in Central
Asia: one is the growing focus by various militant groups
that now see China as an adversary. Another is the risk that
Beijing may inadvertently clash with Moscow's interests in
the region. Finally, there is the longer-term problem of how
China will envisage its role in helping stabilize a region
which has seen growing internal instability and violence over*

the past years. As the increasingly most consequential actor on the ground, China will increasingly be looked to as a player, a role it appears to want to avoid for now.

The narrative of China's engagement with Central Asia and the Caucasus has been one of steady ascension and embrace. There is a clear difference between the two regions from Beijing's perspective, with Central Asia a region which is intimately tied to China, while the Caucasus remains at one remove. The Central Asian relationship was initially marked by concerns and instability, but it has over time developed into an increasingly close relationship. As time has passed, Central Asia has also played an interesting role in Chinese foreign policy thinking, providing an environment in which Beijing can test out new foreign and security policy approaches in a relatively pliant environment. For example, the first international security organization outside UN structures that China was instrumental in creating, the Shanghai Cooperation Organization (SCO), focused on Central Asia. And even more importantly, President Xi Jinping chose to inaugurate his keynote foreign policy concept, the Belt and Road Initiative (BRI), in Astana, Kazakhstan.

The Caucasus occupies a very different role in Chinese foreign policy thinking, something most prominently defined by the fact that the region does not share a direct border with China. As a result, it is largely treated as a potential foreign market, and with the announcement of the Belt and Road Initiative, largely treated as a region which sits at the heart of the network of infrastructure and trade connectivity that BRI represents across the Eurasian heartland.

Reflecting this distinction, this paper will linger more on

the Central Asian relationships, given their higher significance to China. Though it is worth noting that the relationship with the Caucasus is one that is transforming, in large part due to the growing Chinese push in Central Asia which has helped provide an outline of what potential BRI investment can look like, something the countries of the Caucasus are keen to attract. The invasion of Ukraine has impacted this, as discussion of the middle corridor which goes across the Caspian connecting the two regions and bolstering a route of trade for China to Europe, has increased. But we are still in the early days of both, and it remains to be seen what the longer term impact of the war in Ukraine will be on China's relations with the region.

The structure of Chinese engagement with Central Asia can be broken down into four broad areas: economic, cultural, political and security. In fact, the political aspect touches on all of the other three but is worth highlighting separately as there is a quite specific level of engagement at a political level that China has undertaken with the region which is worth noting on its own. However, the central aspect of Chinese engagement with Central Asia which cuts across everything is the importance of Xinjiang in Chinese considerations towards Central Asia. In many ways the sixth Central Asian country (if one places Afghanistan in South Asia), Xinjiang is the primary lens through which China looks at Central Asia and has been regularly at the heart of its engagement and considerations with the region.

Recent Shifts

This focus on Xinjiang is something that has only become more acute in recent times. While Xinjiang has always been a key part of Chinese thinking towards Central Asia, recent difficulties with the region have sharpened Beijing's focus. In contemporary terms, a turning point in Beijing's relations with Xinjiang came in 2009 in the wake of widespread disorder in Urumqi which led to a re-evaluation of policy towards the region. But the policy shifts that followed did not resolve the problems. Violence seemed to escalate over the following years and even spread beyond the region. In 2014, Xi Jinping visited the region, on a tour seemingly focused on bolstering local security efforts, a narrative that was undermined by the detonation of a suicide bomber at Urumqi train station during his visit.

This appears to have provided a green light for China to escalate its security focused approach towards the region. This ratcheted up further in 2016 with the appointment of Chen Quanguo to the role of Party Secretary for Xinjiang. Coming from Tibet, Chen had a reputation as a man who could quell minorities, and he brought with him many of the policies he had developed in Tibet. The result was a widespread escalation of the already pervasive police state throughout Xinjiang. This echoed in Central Asia as some from the co-ethnic communities were caught up in the crackdown, leading to protests in Kazakhstan and Kyrgyzstan in particular. It has led to some tensions at a political level, though for the most part Central Asian governments are cautious to avoid condemning Chinese action at home.

Beijing has also found its security concerns have started to grow regionally in Central Asia as well. In late August 2016, the Chinese Embassy in Bishkek was targeted by a suicide bomber in a plot that was reportedly directed (or at the very least linked) to Uyghur networks in Syria. While this incident was not repeated (and it was not the first time Chinese officials have been targeted in

Kyrgyzstan), it did bring together a number of strands of Chinese concerns. Many of these appear to have focused on Afghanistan in particular, with growing anxiety about Tajikistan in particular being a weak link in the region.

While discussions were likely already underway, by autumn 2016 China formalized an agreement with the Tajik authorities that they would build or refurbish up to 30 or 40 border posts along Tajikistan's border with Afghanistan. In August 2016, China hosted the first session of the Quadrilateral Cooperation and Coordination Mechanism (QCCM) an entity that brought together the Chiefs of Defense Staff of Afghanistan, China, Pakistan and Tajikistan, the grouping that surrounds the Wakhan Corridor, China's physical link to Afghanistan. Reportedly focused on counterterrorism and border security, the QCCM was in many ways a rebuke of the SCO, but also an effort to formalize the PLA's role in the region. In October, this was reaffirmed with a large joint counter-terrorism exercise between Chinese and Tajik forces in Gorno-Badakhshan. Sometime during the year, Tajik officials claim the decision to establish a Chinese base in Tajikistan was also formalized, though the existence of the base is something that is still treated in a somewhat opaque manner by both Chinese and Tajik officials. Its existence is beyond dispute at this point, though it appears to be a People's Armed Police (PAP) base rather than a People's Liberation Army (PLA) base, and it reflects a desire by China to not rely entirely on locals to guarantee its security interests in the region. China has now also built and operates a police special forces training base in Tajikistan, though this appears more traditional military aid than deployment. Chinese private security firms have also started to enter into the region more widely, though for the most part this seems to be focused on Kyrgyzstan where there is a greater degree of concern about personal and business security.

While China has looked more at security in recent years (something accentuated in the wake of the Taliban takeover in Kabul), the economic push into Central Asia has continued. From Beijing's perspective, this is in fact an extension of the security approach. China's ultimate interest is in Xinjiang stability, and they recognize that while a strong security hand can deliver this in the short-term, the longer-term answer is only going to come through economic development and prosperity. Given Xinjiang's landlocked nature, this means a prosperous neighborhood in Central Asia is important as well. Furthermore, interest in the rich natural resource opportunities on offer in the region made China an active player in Central Asia – something that was encouraged by the local governments who sought more investment.

However, recent years have seen a slowdown in investment. While China has steadily risen in the rankings as a trading partner for all of the Central Asian countries, investment from China has in fact slowed down. In part this is in response to broader trends in Chinese outward investment where there has been a push by Beijing to try to ensure greater focus on return on investment and therefore more emphasis on secure projects, it is also a reflection on local tensions and problems that have been generated by key projects. Still, there clearly remains a Chinese appetite for gaining economic benefits from the region. The recent opening of two more wells in Turkmenistan to help grow the volume of natural gas the Chinese National Petroleum Corporation (CNPC) buys from the country is one example at a state-driven level, while the constant level of low-level Chinese private sector investment in

Kyrgyzstan reflects an appetite by Chinese investors to still have a go. That said, the level of investment is generally down. The exception to this is Uzbekistan, where there has been a notable push since the passing of former leader Islam Karimov to try to open the country to more Chinese investment.

All of this stalled abruptly during the pandemic in the face of China's dramatic border closures and COVID-19 restrictions, but seems now to be picking up, with a particular growth in attention in the wake of the war in Ukraine when a number of big projects in the region appear to have become unlocked. The long-delayed Kyrgyz portion of the China-Kyrgyzstan-Uzbekistan railroad now appears to have been approved, while Line D which will help bring the Turkmen gas to China appears to also be moving. It is not clear how much these two are directly linked to events in Ukraine, but Kyrgyz President Sadyr Japarov signaled that Moscow was no longer impeding the project, something relayed to him in conversations with President Putin. Rather than this being about China, however, this was likely an effort by Moscow to try to win some favor in Central Asia highlighting their willingness to encourage more regional connectivity.

A final recent change in China's economic relations with Central Asia is the growing prominence of Chinese online commerce. Chinese technology has long been widely used in the region, including in the building of key infrastructure. But in recent years there has been a notable increase in Chinese online commerce platforms. They have been both growing their presence in the local market, but also increasingly offering Central Asian firms opportunities to sell directly to Chinese consumers. It has also helped displace some of the traditional markets in the region which used to rely on the import and resale of Chinese goods.

Alibaba in particular has followed up on this surge with growing investment in technology and digital platforms in both Central Asia and Russia, including signing multi-billion-dollar investment agreements.

But while the digital and technological environment is a sector in which China has a sharp competitive advantage, the war in Ukraine has highlighted how sensitive the industry is to geopolitics. In the wake of the Russian invasion of Ukraine, AliExpress Russia held a board meeting at which Chinese stakeholder Alibaba announced a cessation of investment into the joint venture that Jack Ma had kicked off to much fanfare and hundreds of millions of investments in 2019. The story since the invasion has been of gradual decline of the firm, including the suspension of sales of some Chinese technical equipment on the platform in Russia out of fears of it turning up on the battlefield in Ukraine. At the same time, Huawei closed down some of its offices in Russia and moved them across the border into Central Asia. Alongside ZTE, HikVision and Dahua, Huawei has been a major provider of telecoms and security technology to Central Asia, it now appears in the wake of the invasion the companies are seeking to increase their presence there to insulate themselves from the risks posed by secondary sanctions against Moscow.

But the key lesson of recent times is that while China still sees economic opportunities from Central Asia as important, it prioritizes its security concerns in Xinjiang and as a result lets the relationship be heavily influenced by Urumqi, or defines things along the lines of how they will impact Xinjiang. This low prioritization by Beijing in its strategic thinking is not unique to Central Asia – Zhongnanhai largely focuses almost single-mindedly on the relationship with the United States as the priority.

But the general hesitation is something that was highlighted again recently in discussions over Afghanistan. While Beijing spent time visiting all of the relevant Central Asian players, it does not seem to have stepped forward to provide much by way of leadership since the Taliban takeover and only limited economic and humanitarian support. Rather, Beijing has focused on its own particular interests in Afghanistan, hedging in its relationships with the new authorities and emphasized blaming the U.S. for what has taken place. While this narrative is not new, its particular sharpness emphasizes the degree to which China has increasingly decided to see everything through the lens of its great power competition with the United States. For Central Asia, however, it is frustrating to have Beijing – Afghanistan's wealthiest and most influential neighbor – continue to hedge in a situation where they are clearly concerned about what the future holds. Central Asian officials have found the Chinese to be amongst the most active lobbyists for the Taliban in multilateral forums, in a likely attempt to get someone else to formally acknowledge the Taliban's authority first as well as a way of currying favor with the Taliban. The policy approach seems to be working with the Taliban who seem happy to continue to champion Beijing as one of their important partners.

Looking across the Caspian, in the Caucasus, there is a very limited security relationship to speak of with the countries and little evidence of Beijing pushing to get involved. China for the most part wants to avoid entanglements or trying to act as a broker in clashes between the various regional powers. The economic motivation to engage in the Caucasus is there, and Georgia in particular has warmly embraced the BRI concept, going so far as to sign a Free Trade Agreement with Beijing in 2016. Both

Azerbaijan and Armenia are also willing partners in the BRI, but the overall size of the region and its resources is relatively limited and does not have the same physical links to China, or Uyghur related security concerns that justify an enhanced attention. As a result, what engagement there has been has tended to be at a lower level, with Chinese regions (like Xinjiang) leading in relations, and specific companies pushing in to reap opportunities they see. The degree of state coordination and direction behind all of this is unclear.

President Xi Jinping's 2022 visit to Central Asia, his first trip outside China since the pandemic, highlighted another element to China's security relations with the region. This was visible in the commentary around his stop in Kazakhstan, where President Xi spoke of China's support for "Kazakhstan in safeguarding national independence, sovereignty and territorial integrity." Locally, this was interpreted as being a signal that China would step to defend Kazakhstan should Russia decide to make a move against the country. Other rumors circulating around the region suggest that China was responsible for pressuring Russia to remove its troops from Kazakhstan in the wake of the invasion. The overall point being that there is a growing sentiment in the region that China might be an alternative security protector to Moscow. Yet, while this optimism exists in the region, and appears to have been fanned by Russian adventurism in Ukraine, there is little evidence that it has translated into tangible action by China.

China's Views on Central Asia and the Caucasus

Traditionally, Beijing has seen Central Asia and the Caucasus through a Russian lens. Chinese experts looking at the region tend to speak Russian, and constantly refer to the fact that Beijing would not do anything in the region without consulting their Russian partners. China sees the region as part of a wider former Soviet belt, though there is a clear distinction in interest and attention with regards to Central Asia as opposed to the Caucasus or Central and Eastern Europe. While in diplomatic staffing terms, it seems as though China treats the region as a single space (diplomats are shuffled between posts) this is likely a reflection of linguistic requirements more than anything else. Central Asia does seem to register as a higher priority than the other areas – though Central and Eastern Europe has developed as a point of interest for Beijing given its role in China-Europe relations, and their close link to the U.S.

In practical terms, China has distinct approaches to each country in Central Asia and is able to impose its views to varying degrees. In Turkmenistan, the opaque nature of the country is something that confuses China as much as anyone else, though it is clear that given the importance of Chinese energy-related income, Ashgabat treats Beijing as a closer partner than others. Beijing does not appear very preoccupied with the closed nature of the country as it has continued to deliver on the energy requirements China wants, though even CNPC has struggled to manage the Turkmen banking system, a reality that illustrates the difficulty of operating within the country. China sees Turkmenistan largely as an opportunity, a perspective that does not appear to have changed much over the past decades, though it has not been without frustrations for Beijing along the way. The Turkmen in turn are not thrilled at being reliant on China as their main customer and have sought (and thus far for the most part failed) to diversify. This is something Beijing has observed passively. The recent moves to build a fourth pipeline bringing Turkmen gas to

China highlights how there is a clear acceptance on both sides about the relationship.

Kazakhstan and Uzbekistan are seen by Beijing as significant enough players that Beijing is willing to accord them with considerable respect and appear to engage them on the terms they want to be engaged. Beijing views Uzbekistan as a potential opportunity, and China recognizes both the economic opportunity and the relevance of Tashkent as a regional power broker and player. In Kazakhstan, China long played to the country's sense of power and influence, though it has also on occasion sought to push its interests in more strident terms behind closed doors. China and Kazakhstan have managed, however, to keep these tensions out of the headlines, though the bubbling Sinophobia that is visible in the country is often used by political players to cause trouble and has placed practical difficulties on companies operating in the country. This in addition to the fact that some of the angriest expressions regionally towards China's crackdown in Xinjiang can be found in Kazakhstan have created some tensions. However, both governments seem keen to try to keep them under control.

Finally, Kyrgyzstan and Tajikistan are seen in a similar basket by Beijing as powers that are largely *demandeurs* in their relationship with Beijing. China is rapidly becoming their most significant economic partner, and Beijing has little sense of confidence in their ability to deliver on security outcomes within their borders which address Chinese concerns. This is reflected in a growing bilateral security relationship, as well as a willingness by Chinese officials to throw their weight around in bilateral engagements. At the same time, Beijing is unable to control local sentiment which is increasingly anti-Chinese in both countries, something that has caused some friction for Chinese investors – in particular in Kyrgyzstan.

This state of relations is largely reflective of the broader trajectory over time of China's relations with the region. They have stayed fairly static, though the pandemic hit the bilateral economic relations substantially given China's abrupt and severe lockdown. It is also notable that in terms of trade at least, the passing of Uzbekistan President Islam Karimov opened Uzbekistan to China in a dramatic way. In all of the other countries, the current approach is largely an extension of how China has seen the country for the past few years, with growing Chinese confidence and wealth often being the main change.

The key external issue for Beijing with the region, however, is not really within the region, but rather with Moscow, where China's growing influence in Central Asia has over time created a greater sense of tension. While it is clear that Russia still has some very strong levers of influence that surpass China's, there is an awareness in Beijing that there is some sensitivity here with regards Moscow. And Russia in turn appears to have a sense of concern that the region could become an entry point for unfettered Chinese investment and influence into their domestic economy. At the same time, this awareness and sensitivity has not slowed any Chinese initiatives. And it is possible that now that pandemic restrictions are lifted and the Russian economy more generally finds itself in a more precarious position in the wake of the invasion of Ukraine, we are likely to see an acceleration of Chinese trade and investment.

Overall, however, Central Asia does not register very high in Beijing's broader considerations. This was most clearly shown recently in the Ministry of Foreign Affair's willingness during the pandemic to amplify rumors started by Russian authorities about bioweapons labs that had been given U.S. government support in the post-Soviet space, including some in Kazakhstan, might be the source of COVID-19. This alongside a series of articles that were widely disseminated in the Chinese media in 2020 which appeared to suggest that Central Asian countries were not in fact independent countries, but rather provinces of China, all served to highlight the reality that Beijing spends very little time thinking in much of a considered way about how Central Asia sees China. The assumption from Beijing is that these powers will always want and need a relationship with China, meaning Beijing can largely proceed as it wants.

China's priority with Central Asia is Xinjiang. This is the case in terms of the region's potential as a place where dissidents can gather to threaten China, or in terms of the region causing problems for China's domestic security and economic stability approach. Within this context, the two priority countries are Kazakhstan and Kyrgyzstan, both of which share borders with China and also have substantial Uyghur diaspora, in addition to the ethnic Kazakh and Kyrgyz communities in Xinjiang. Kazakh-stan also has the distinction of being an important source of imported natural resources, both in hydrocarbon as well as mineral terms. It is also the main conduit for the major transport routes from China to Europe along the Belt and Road. This elevates the country to some degree above the others.

In the Caucasus, the calculation is different. In many ways, the Caucasus is simply another foreign region with which it needs to engage and consequently it is treated as such. The BRI is a major consideration with the region, given its location at the heart of where many of the routes across the Eurasian landmass would flow. In dealing with the countries, China is always conscious of the Russian relationship, and is more likely to defer to Moscow than it necessarily would in Central Asia. The region has tried to use China as a card to play in its wider geopolitical struggles with Russia, or the west. But Beijing has little interest in getting dragged into these clashes, and engages at a utilitarian level.

Russia is the only power that Beijing considers a genuine competitor in Central Asia. And even there, it is largely seen through the lens of cooperation at a more strategic level, where Beijing is more focused on its larger relationship with Moscow than its more limited relations with the Central Asian capitals. With the Caucasus the calculation is even stronger, with even fewer reasons for China to not defer to Russian concerns. The only interesting wrinkle to this is the Russian war with Georgia in 2008 which was an act which Beijing was not happy about – suggesting as it did a world order in which neighbors could recognize minority communities and then use them as a context to invade. The precedent set by Moscow was one Beijing did not appreciate, and expressed displeasure about, though stopped short of open condemnation of Moscow. This anxiety was reflected again in 2014 with the first Russian incursion into Ukraine, and more recently with the second major Russian invasion – though Beijing has become far less openly condemnatory in its posture towards Moscow as time has passed, a reflection of the wider strategic relationship becoming closer. These events did not change Beijing's broader strategic calculus towards the region though it did emphasize the broader awkwardness of the relationship with Moscow.

The recent invasion of Ukraine appears to be something that Beijing is more willing than previous Russian actions to move quickly beyond. From China's perspective, while the precedent that is set is not good, nor are the apocalyptic threats about nuclear conflict emanating from Moscow, they do not feel in a position to do anything to condemn Moscow. What opportunities might arise in terms of growing Chinese influence in third locations like Central Asia or the Caucasus will be taken, but there is little evidence of China rushing in to fill a void. Rather Beijing wants to continue to move forward, steadily growing in influence and interests in the region, largely in parallel or maybe now even in coordination with Moscow. The mention of Central Asia in particular in the joint statement to be issued after President Xi and President Putin's Summit in Moscow in 2023 highlighted how far the collective position on the region had come.

When looking to other capitals, Beijing has entertained opportunities for cooperation with Europe (through joint projects between Chinese entities and the European Bank for Reconstruction and Development and broader discussions about possible Belt and Road cooperation) and its energy firms have entered into large-scale consortia with other international energy companies in the region. China has cooperated in the past with both India and the United States bilaterally in Afghanistan, but there has been little evidence of much desire to expand such cooperation in Central Asia. There has been some cooperation with Turkish intelligence in the region, though this has been on narrow concerns. At a strategic level, it is not clear how much Beijing focuses on Turkey, Iran or individual European actors within the region. With Turkey in particular, there is an awkward undertone to the relationship in the form of Ankara's support and close relations to the Uyghur cause, which ties the country directly to a problem within China that is a major concern to the authorities.

China has also played a role in advancing the Shanghai Cooperation Organization (SCO) as a major regional institution in which all of the Central Asian powers, except Turkmenistan, have membership and extra-regional powers India, Pakistan and Russia are members, with others like Iran, Afghanistan, Belarus, Mongolia or Sri Lanka have some stake. Yet, China's treatment of the SCO is in some ways exemplary of its broader willingness to work with others in Central Asia. Beijing never seems to reject engagement, but this is not always followed by action. The decision to create a Central Asia 5 plus China format – which echoes previous Japanese, European and American formats – highlights another of these platforms which so far have not produced much action or opportunity.

This is a reflection of China's sense of confidence in the region, where Beijing for the most part seems to assume a level unassailable importance which is ultimately going to trump all others. The one power they see as a potential competitor is Moscow, but there China recognizes that the overall geostrategic relationship is more significant than Central Asia meaning that for the time being, it will not entirely disregard Russia's wishes and Moscow is similarly unlikely to cause too much of a fuss.

The Future

China's influence and engagement with Central Asia and the Caucasus is likely to continue on an upward trajectory over the next five years, picking up in particular after the COVID-19 blip (which has only recently been lifted in Chinese terms). Events in Afghanistan have created a new level of potential uncertainty, but China's unwillingness to step forward into a role of responsibility or leadership highlights the likelihood that Beijing will simply continue to hedge in Afghanistan going forwards. Even in the event of eventual recognition of the Taliban government, it is unlikely that China will pour in vast sums of investment or strengthen its security presence, but rather it will seek to continue to invest in securing its secondary borders with the country – principally in Tajikistan and Pakistan. This might extend to Uzbekistan (though likely unnecessary) and possibly Turkmenistan (though Ashgabat is likely to continue to be highly reticent in this regard).

The dilemma, however, will be if Uyghur networks are able to reestablish themselves in any great strength in Afghanistan either under Taliban protection or take advantage of an unstable environment in the country. Beyond this as well, there has been a notable refocusing by various militant groups across the region towards treating China as an adversary. The Islamic State in Khorasan Province (ISKP) recently launched an attack in which they specifically menaced China's cooperation with the Taliban government. This comes atop an increasing rate of attacks against Chinese nationals by separatists and jihadists in Pakistan. All of this might force Beijing's hand, though it is still not clear that China would abandon its current view of Afghanistan as a "Graveyard of Empires." Rather, it is likely that Beijing would find other local actors to engage with to manage its problems. These could come from within the various factions in Afghanistan, Pakistan or Central Asia.

The relationships with the Caucasus are likely to going to continue to grow, and it is the one with Georgia that probably bears closest watching. The country has made itself the most welcoming towards Chinese investment, something that has been done to specifically help Tbilisi hedge against western abandonment and Russian incursion. It will be an interesting strategic question to see how Beijing comes out should Moscow try something again, and the relationship might become an interesting bellwether of the broader China-Russia relationship. In that, should Moscow start to do something in Georgia which damages Chinese firms, endangers nationals, or again sets a new norm in international behavior Beijing is not happy with, it will be interesting to see how the two manage the situation.

The Russian invasion of Ukraine has shaken the deck up across Eurasia, and in Central Asia and the Caucasus in particular, though it is not so far clear how much Beijing will actually seek to take advantage of this situation rather than continue forward in much the same way that it was. The sometimes exaggerated narratives that can be found in western discourse around the China-Russia balance in the region seem to miss the reality on the ground that China has largely stayed on a steady and upward trajectory that focuses on their interests notwithstanding whatever issues play out on the ground. The Russian invasion of Ukraine has created some uncertainty, but it is not clear how much Beijing will take advantage of this in some specific way, rather than simply move forward and find a more receptive environment. The decision by Kazakhstan and possibly others to lift visa restrictions for Chinese nationals highlights how the region clearly values Chinese engagement, and this pliant environment is something that China no doubt sees and recognizes it can continue to foster with relatively little effort and without needing to particularly make any aggressive moves against Moscow.

With regards Central Asia, the greatest potential risk to Beijing's future in the region is that it lets its growing hubris get ahead of itself to the point that it entirely overlooks Moscow's concerns in particular. While until now Russia has seemed willing to simply let China sweep in, events in Afghanistan have highlighted to Moscow once again the need to have direct presence and influence in the region. And this needs to be done with effective coordination with Beijing. Should Beijing continue to expand its influence unabated in Central Asia and start to use the region as a staging point for greater economic penetration into Russia that starts to look like it might be undermining Moscow's control, it is possible that a clash could take place. While at the moment the geopolitical sands are aligned towards Beijing and Moscow staying in lockstep in confrontation with the west, the question for the future will be whether China starts to take this for granted or its hubris gets the best of calculations that recognize Russia's contribution to its interests in the region. Whatever the case, Beijing will be a significant (if not the most significant) actor in Central Asia, but it will be a much more complicated ascent if it is done in an antagonistic manner with Moscow.

Russian Strategy Towards the Caucasus and Central Asia: A Dominant Power on Defense?

Ariel Cohen

In the thirty years since the collapse of the Soviet Union, the Russian Federation has sought to reassert its regional dominance over its neighbors through both direct confrontation and soft power. Despite the country's progress with consolidating its sphere of influence, which includes the January 2022 CSTO deployment in Kazakhstan, Moscow's goal of regional hegemony is far from assured. Everything will ride on the outcome of Putin's re-invasion of Ukraine. The military setbacks, the rise of China, radical trans-national Islam, the potential spill-over of Taliban ascendancy in Afghanistan, and maturing of post-Soviet nation-states present roadblocks to Russian ambitions. Moscow must carefully manage its interactions with Beijing, keep Turkey, Islamism and Taliban in check, stabilize the Western front, manage increasingly hostile relations with the West, and respect nationhood in the Caucasus and Central Asia. It is a tall order.

Since the dissolution of the USSR and the birth of the modern-day Russian Federation, Russia has gone to great lengths to reassert its post-imperial influence in the now independent post-Soviet Republics of Central Asia and the Southern Caucasus. The years immediately following the collapse of the Soviet system were defined by ethnic conflicts in Abkhazia, Chechnya, Nagorno-Karabakh, South Ossetia, and Tajikistan, with Russian leadership seeking to play the role of either suppressor, mediator, or agitator – whichever suited its interests – to become the region's hegemon, at times in the guise of the guarantor of stability and security. When it failed, it used force: in 2008 in Georgia, in 2014 in the Crimea and Donbass, and now throughout Ukraine.

The past 30 years have seen Russian regional power projection take many shapes, including support of aggressive irredentism and limited wars in Ukraine, Moldova, Georgia, and Chechnya – and most recently, leading a Collective Security Treaty Organization (CSTO) military deployment in Kazakhstan that saw the deployment of over 3,500 Russian troops. The war in Ukraine opened a new page in the six-century saga of Russian imperialism. Pursuing an informal empire where possible, and direct intervention where necessary, over the past five years, Kremlin strategy has shifted away from direct confrontation with neighbors towards proxy involvement, producing asymmetric tactical advantages at low costs.

South Caucasus: Conflict Mountains

The armistice brokered by Russia in the 2020 Nagorno-Karabakh conflict was a demonstration of Russia's success in achieving geostrategic goals through deft diplomatic maneuvering. Despite Armenia's heavy economic and security dependence on Russia, the Kremlin wanted to punish Nikol Pashinyan, who came to power on the crest of the Velvet Revolution of 2018 and expressed the pro-European sentiment common to a part of the Armenian political elite.[1] The Kremlin further calculated that the geopolitical center of gravity was shifting away from its client state and towards Azerbaijan. One can only speculate about the private agreements between Russian President Vladimir Putin and his Azerbaijani counterpart.

During the 2020 conflict, Russia held back support for its intransigent alley, knowing that Armenia had little choice in the matter and gambling that Azerbaijan would view its (in)action with gratitude. This allowed Russia to "have its geopolitical cake and eat it too."[2] The ploy worked. Armenia's lack of alternatives combined with Azerbaijan's clear military advantage in the conflict ultimately allowed the Kremlin to broker a ceasefire that permitted the stationing of Russian peacekeeping troops in the region for the next five years – a geopolitical victory.

To Russia's South, as Georgia is commemorating the 13th anniversary of the August War of 2008, it is still recovering from the political and economic damage incurred by the conflict, which began with Russian support for secessionist movements in Abkhazia and South Ossetia in the early 1990s and culminated in a Russian invasion. Lack of security guarantees by the West, despite overtures from Tbilisi for NATO membership, emboldened the Kremlin to take military action. It did so successfully. To

1   Kendrick Foster, "Armenia's Velvet Revolution: Lessons from the Caucasus." Harvard International Review, May 29, 2019. https://hir.harvard.edu/armenias-velvet-revolution/

2   Nicu Popescu. "A captive ally: Why Russia isn't rushing to Armenia's aid." European Council on Foreign Relations, October 8, 2020. https://ecfr.eu/article/a_captive_ally_why_russia_isnt_rushing_to_armenias_aid/

this day the war has displaced over 20,000 citizens[3] and completely severed diplomatic relations. Russia pursues its long-term strategy of "borderization" with Georgia – turning occupied territories into Russian military bases and gradually pushing border markers into Georgian territory.[4] While Russia fully considers Georgia a part of its "natural" sphere of influence, the Kremlin's actions have had a galvanizing effect on the Georgian populace fanning pro-Euro Atlantic aspirations.

Central Asia: Between the Bear and the Dragon

Across the Caspian, Russia maintains generally positive relations with the Central Asian states, particularly in security matters. Kazakhstan, Kyrgyzstan, and Turkmenistan are co-members with Russia, Belarus, and Armenia in the recently deployed CSTO, as well as the Shanghai Cooperation Organization (SCO) which also includes Uzbekistan.

Diplomatic relations with Kazakhstan have historically been strong, with recent events underscoring the depth of bilateral ties. President Kassym-Jomart Tokayev's demonstrated his trust in the Kremlin when he requested the deployment of Russian and CSTO peacekeepers following the New Year protests. It remains to be seen whether in the long term, Russia's involvement would trigger Kazakh nationalism, and if it solves more problems for Russia than it creates.

Prior to CSTO deployment, however, Russian-Kazakh relations were entering a period of cooling. Recent comments by the

---

3   Ban Ki-moon. "Status of internally displaced persons and refugees from Abkhazia, Georgia, and the Tskhinvali region/ South Ossetia, Georgia." *United Nations General Assembly: Report of the Secretary-General*, May 7, 2014. https://www.un.org/ga/search/view_doc.asp?symbol=A/68/868

4   Natia Seskuria, "Russia's "Hybrid Aggression" against Georgia: The Use of Local and External Tools." *Center for Strategic & International Studies*, September 21, 2021. https://www.csis.org/analysis/russias-hybrid-aggression-against-georgia-use-local-and-external-tools

Russian Duma members that Kazakhstan's territory was a Russian "gift" and interference in Kazakhstan's language policy resulted in domestic backlash.[5]

Russia is a major economic player in the region, with relationships built on remittances, investment, and commodity trade. Kazakhstan and Kyrgyzstan are members along with Russia in the Eurasian Economic Union (EEU) while Uzbekistan is an EEU observer, and Tajikistan's potential membership is being discussed. In addition to security cooperation, close economic ties support Russia's belief that Central Asia remains a part of its sphere of influence. Since the dissolution of the USSR a significant portion of Russia's labor force, especially in the blue-collar segment of construction, sanitation, agriculture, etc., has been shaped by net migration from Central Asia and the Caucasus. Particularly early on, temporary and permanent labor migration were difficult to distinguish, exacerbated by porous borders and unresolved citizenship for those bearing Soviet-era passports. In the early 2000s, some experts estimated between 3 and 5 million illegal immigrants residing in Russia,[6] with at least 1 million remaining today.[7]

Russia's greatest obstacle in Central Asia is China's Belt and Road Initiative, with Beijing's investment into infrastructure and energy projects dwarfing what Moscow can offer.[8] The creation of a trading empire in and across Russia's geopolitical front yard

---

5   Petr Trotsenko, "Controversial 'Russian Gift' Comments Spark Mixed Feelings in Northern Kazakhstan." *Radio Free Europe/Radio Liberty*, January 5, 2021. https://www.rferl.org/a/kazakh-russian-gift-comments/31035059.html

6   Natalia Vlasova, "Есть ли альтернатива гастарбайтерам?" - Yest' li al'ternativa gastarbaiteram ("Is there an altnerantive to Gastarbeiters?") International Labour Organization, 2016. https://www.ilo.org/wcmsp5/groups/public/---europe/---ro-geneva/---sro-moscow/documents/publication/wcms_308948.pdf

7   Elena Teslova, "Russia demands 1M illegal migrants to leave country." *Anadolu Agency*, April 17, 2021. https://www.aa.com.tr/en/world/russia-demands-1m-illegal-migrants-to-leave-country/2211717

8   Reid Standish, "China's Central Asian Plans Are Unnerving Moscow." *Foreign Policy*, December 23, 2019. https://foreignpolicy.com/2019/12/23/china-russia-central-asia-competition/

has created an uneven relationship. Russia cannot compete with China economically and notably benefits from the development brought on by their investment, but allowing China too great an influence threatens to not only pull Russia's neighbors into its immense orbit but Russia as well.[9]

Russia's Geopolitical Challenges

Comparison between Russia's neo-imperial aspirations and reality expose a mixed picture. Russia was still strong security-wise before the February 2022 re-invasion of Ukraine, but now questions mount over its long term power. The threats, especially from radical Islam, Afghanistan, and China, are rising – and Russia may be losing economic competition to China.

Russia's current challenges in the region are three-fold: 1) stave off the defeat in Ukraine 2) provide the security and stability it promises within its claimed sphere; and 2) the task of warding off the economic incursions of rival powers such as the United States, EU, and China. Within its own borders, Russia faces a threat from Islamist ideology and radical terrorist cells, among them Chechen Islamists whose calls for "holy war" in the North Caucasus helped trigger the Second Chechen War. In the 1990s, the Taliban and Al Qaeda recognized the Chechen state to the Kremlin's chagrin.[10] Moscow is aware of the Islamic threat emanating from Central Asia including Afghanistan, but resists creating a "hard" border between itself and the region.

Presently, the Head of the Chechen Republic, Ramzan

---

9   Paul Stronski and Nicole, "Cooperation and Competition: Russia and China in Central Asia, the Russian Far East, and the Arctic." *Carnegie Endowment for International Peace*, Feb. 28, 2018. https://carnegieendowment.org/2018/02/28/cooperation-and-competition-russia-and-china-in-central-asia-russian-far-east-and-arctic-pub-75673

10 Thomas D. Grant, "Current Development: Afghanistan Recognizes Chechnya." *American University International Law Review*, vol. 15 no. 4, 2000. https://digitalcommons.wcl.american.edu/cgi/viewcontent.cgi?referer=&httpsredir=1&article=1276&context=auilr

Kadyrov, whose cult of personality manifests itself in the ubiquitous portraits found throughout Chechnya, rules with an iron grip – like his father before him, the assassinated President Hajj Akhmad Kadyrov.

Ostensibly a Putin loyalist in a de-jure Russian territory, Kadyrov has tremendous sway over his realm and has had his own territorial ambitions rooted in the messy 1992 split of the Chechen-Ingush Autonomous Republic into two Muslim-majority republics. Kadyrov led a relatively unsuccessful expeditionary force in Ukraine, which now appears to be replaced by the Wagner Private Military Company.

In 2018, Kadyrov orchestrated an unbalanced land exchange with Ingushetia, where the unpopular deal and perception of Kremlin favoritism resulting in considerable discontent.[11] The region continues to see sporadic fighting in its more mountainous areas, due to a practical lack of security control, and remains Russia's poorest region. Protecting its interests over the North Caucasus will be necessary if the Kremlin wishes to portray itself as the regional hegemon and a viable protector of its constituent republics and allies. Similarly, Russia's work to prevent spillover violence from Taliban-ruled Afghanistan into Central Asia will be another test of its regional dominance.

Islamists also penetrate Russia's aspirational sphere of influence that is quite porous, which raises questions about security, smuggling, contraband, and exports of extremism. Since the Islamic State's terrorist threat against the 2018 FIFA Games, Russia has carefully watched for spread of Islamist ideals and

---

11 Morgan Henson, "Chechen-Ingush Land Dispute: A Policy Primer." *Geohistory*, Dec. 8, 2018. https://geohistory.today/chechen-ingush-land-dispute/

threats from abroad.[12] Still, considerable investment opportunities exist in Central Asia and the North Caucasus, particularly in terms of infrastructure, energy trade, manufacturing, and services. Yet, it is doubtful that in view of the war and the ensuing sanctions, Moscow has capital resources to successfully invest in these regions.

Beijing and Moscow have benefited from a near-lack of American competition in Central Asia due a historically scattered foreign policy and development approach, exacerbated by geographic distance. U.S.-Kazakhstan trade totaled $2.25 billion in 2019 compared to $19.67 billion for Russia in the same year.[13] Comparatively, China's total trade with Kazakhstan in the same year accounted for $14. 39 billion.[14]

China's Belt and Road Initiative (BRI), a multi-trillion-dollar infrastructural framework for a 21st century Silk Road trading empire, represents a long-term and real threat to Russian imperial aspirations. Initially announced in 2013 at the Nazarbayev University in Astana, a $2 trillion, it is a 30-year program plans to "reformat" all of the Eastern Hemisphere. Beijing has long been providing ready access to credit lines for the funding of national and transnational transportation and energy projects across Central Asia, with a particular interest in funding renewable energy projects, and acquiring fossil fuels, uranium, and critical minerals – the backbone of 21st century economic development.[15] Several regional oil and gas pipelines have been built in the last

---

12 Mariya Omelicheva, "The Nature and Sources of Terrorist Threat in Russia: An "Armed Underground" or ISIL?." *Ponars Eurasia*, Nov. 26, 2018. https://www.ponarseurasia.org/the-nature-and-sources-of-terrorist-threat-in-russia-an-armed-underground-or-isil/

13 "Kazakhstan: Trade Statistics." *Global Edge*. https://globaledge.msu.edu/countries/kazakhstan/tradestats

14 Ibid.

15 Lea Melnikovová, "China's interests in Central Asian economies" *Human Affairs*, vol. 30 no. 2, 2020. www.degruyter.com/document/doi/10.1515/humaff-2020-0022/html

two decades to meet China's ever-increasing thirst for energy.[16] Kazakhstan, Central Asia's largest economy and often referred to as the "buckle" of the BRI, is embracing the connectivity and prosperity of closer ties to China.[17] The Central Asian states benefit greatly from their exports of fuels, minerals, agricultural goods and other products to China, presenting an obstacle to Russia insofar as their interests those of the rising great power are aligned. As Russia's strategic and economic power is spent in Ukraine, China's mettle rises along its periphery, including in Central Asia. Therefore, Russia's defeat suits China, as does its victory.

Russian Lens: Geopolitical Aspirations

In opposing foreign influence and bolstering its own from a position of financial disadvantage, Russia must rely on its preexisting relations to regional leaders. In publications issued by pro-Kremlin think tanks, Russia alleges to approach diplomacy on a bilateral basis, and as a collective bound by the Commonwealth of Independent States (CIS) Treaty.[18] The CIS was organized in the early days of the post-Soviet era in an attempt to recoup some regional unity and confirm Russian leadership. In the three decades since, the importance of the alliance has waned in comparison to direct diplomacy, though it remains closely bound to Russia, as well as the foundation of multiple economic and military agreements.

As Russia determines its geopolitical priorities through the prism of the war in Ukraine, security and economic issues are at the forefront, with a willingness to re-evaluate priorities and

---

16 VNBK. "Central Asia-China Gas Pipeline - 10 Years." *National Oil and Gas Service Association*, Jn. 7, 2020. https://nangs.org/news/world/gazoprovodu-tsentralynaya-aziya-kitay-10-let

17 Bolat Nurgaliev, "China's Belt Road: Kazakhstan and Geopolitics." *Kazinform*, June 2, 2020. https://www.inform.kz/ru/kitayskiy-poyas-put-kazakhstan-i-geopolitika_a3656882

18 Ulugbek Khasanov, "Central Asia: Regional Security as a Process", Valdai Club, Jul. 15, 2021. https://ru.valdaiclub.com/a/highlights/tsentralnaya-aziya-regionalnaya-bezopasnost/

relations, should they cease to make strategic sense. This can be observed in the case of the Nagorno-Karabakh War, where the longstanding relationship with Armenia was set aside in favor of accommodating Azerbaijan and Turkey. While it is commonly argued that the change was a political response to Putin's frustration with Armenia's 2018 Velvet Revolution that saw pro-Russian President Serzh Sargsyan removed – undeniably a factor – equally as significant was Azerbaijan's straightforward superior economic and military power, coupled with Baku's alignment with Russia's regional rival Turkey. Were Russia inflexible in its perception and handling of its alliances, any hopes of regional leadership would likely be dead in the water.

The Collective Security Treaty Organization (CSTO) remains a key framework for post-Soviet Eurasian military cooperation, and a tool for the exercise of Russian power with the consent of other signatories. Unlike NATO, the CSTO until January 2022 had never deployed peacekeepers to a conflict zone, even when requested to do so, as in the case of the 2010 ethnic violence in southern Kyrgyzstan.[19] When confronted with Kazakhstan's request for a deployment of peacekeepers following the violence of early January 2022, however, the CSTO under President Putin's leadership immediately deployed troops to safeguard critical infrastructure and support Kazakh security services. There exists no unified strategy for the response of the CSTO states to internal or international conflicts. Rather, until now it was primarily used to facilitate the preferential transfer of military equipment and to modernize military standards. CSTO specifically acted as a transitionary tool of military cooperation from the early post-Soviet

---

19 Miriam Elder, "Kyrgyzstan tests Russia's regional commitments." *Agence France-Presse,* June 15, 2010. https://www.pri.org/stories/2010-06-15/kyrgyzstan-tests-russias-regional-commitments

era to the present day.[20] CSTO proved its futility in the latest bout of fighting in Ukraine.

Yet, post-Soviet loyalties fray slowly. Even the most prosperous of the independent post-Soviet states (excluding the Baltic NATO/EU members), Kazakhstan has maintained fairly positive relations with Russia despite a willingness to strengthen economic and diplomatic ties with China, the EU, and the United States as part of the multi-vector foreign policy championed by its first President Nursultan Nazarbayev. CSTO troop pullout is complete, with Russian Defense Minister Sergei Shoigu asserting that the process should take 7-10 days.[21] However, President Tokayev clearly distanced himself from the Kremlin's position on Ukraine, reiterating non-recognition of the Crimea and Donbass annexation. Kazakhstan does all it can to observe the western sanctions.

Russia's position as a security guarantor of the region is being tested post-Afghanistan, and that position is threatened by Chinese investment in Central Asia since the early 2010s, particularly as Russia can no longer claim a virtual monopoly on arms sales. In terms of economic dominance, Russian annual trade with Central Asia stands at $28.65 billion, two thirds of Beijing's $46.48 billion.[22] By comparison, Russian accounted for 80 percent of the region's trade in the 1990s ($110 billion).[23] The long-term outlook for Russian economic competition with China in the region remains grim.

---

20 Navruz Karimov, "Effectiveness of the CSTO in the context of the changing regional security system." *Central Asian Bureau for Analytical Reporting*, Jan. 11, 2021. https://cabar.asia/en/effectiveness-of-the-csto-in-the-context-of-the-changing-regional-security-system

21 "Russia-Led CSTO Troops Begin Withdrawal From Kazakhstan" *Radio Free Europe Liberty Radio*, Jan. 13, 2022. https://www.rferl.org/a/kazakhstan-csto-troops-withdrawal-russia/31652147.html

22 "Get Insights by Country" Global Edge. *https://globaledge.msu.edu/global-insights/by/country*

23 Edward Lemon, "How is Russia Responding to China's Creeping Security Presence in Tajikistan?" *Russian Analytical Digest,* March 6, 2020. https://css.ethz.ch/content/dam/ethz/special-interest/gess/cis/center-for-securities-studies/pdfs/RAD_248.pdf

Afghanistan: The Cauldron of Chaos

If there is a singular inflection point which might make or break Russian dreams, the American withdrawal from Afghanistan – and the ensuing power vacuum – may be it. America's hasty and messy abandonment of the two-decades-long conflict has seen the Taliban, Al Qaeda, ISIS-K and other radical organizations reemerge as geopolitical players and turn Afghanistan yet again into a fertile territory for Islamic extremism. Russia has put on a calm front, built up contacts with Taliban, and avoided military moves to invite conflict with the Taliban, perhaps remembering their last jaunt into the graveyard of empires which lasted a decade and contributed to the fall of the Soviet Union.

Yet, Russia appears to have a willingness to engage with the region and is openly communicating with the Taliban. Open diplomatic channels have been paired with military exercises alongside Tajikistan and Uzbekistan on the Afghan borders, as well as meetings between Shanghai Cooperation Organization and CSTO members and other powers demonstrating an awareness of the security threat posed by the terrorist-run state.[24] Putin has been an early voice against accepting Afghan refugees, noting the lack of a filtering mechanism to prevent a potential influx of Islamists, thus drawing a wedge in the relations between Washington and its Central Asian friends, and thwarting U.S. requests to accommodate refugees in the neighboring Central Asian states.

America's withdrawal provided an opportunity for Russia to make a case to all of its neighbors, the Central Asian states in particular, that the United States is not capable of providing security and is not a reliable ally. And while geographic distance allows

---

24   Tina Dolbaia and Michael Robinson, "Russia, Turkey, and Iran: Regional Powers React to U.S. Withdrawal from Afghanistan." *Walsh School of Foreign Service*, 2021. ceres.georgetown.edu/research/student-projects/russia-turkey-and-iran-regional-powers-react-to-u-s-withdrawal-from-afghanistan/

many U.S. policymakers to put Afghanistan out of their minds, chronic instability there is an enormous threat for the war-torn country's neighbors – and will pose secondary and tertiary consequences for U.S. foreign policy in Eurasia. Russia can make the case for a strengthened CSTO and perhaps achieve some success as a result of the fall of Kabul. Reports that the Pentagon was interested in monitoring Afghanistan from Russian military bases may demonstrate an awareness in Washington that abandoning each and every regional foothold was a grave error that has given Russia, at least for now, the opportunity to dominate the region's security and intelligence.[25]

For countries who face Russian aggression, bruised faith in American assistance might leave them more willing to give in, particularly if they view themselves and their sovereignty as lower priorities to the U.S. than East Asia and the Pacific. In October 2021, a Taliban delegation arrived arrive in Moscow for talks on Afghanistan alongside China, Pakistan, India, and Iran. The U.S was not invited. This was a shrewd Kremlin move to be viewed as a regional power broker.[26]

Conclusion: Challenges to Moscow Grow

As the 2020s march on, it was in Russia's best interest to carefully compete and collaborate with China, while keeping Islamism in check and ensuring that the Taliban does not destabilize Central Asia. This came to an end when Putin desperately courted China's support for his war adventure in Ukraine. So far, Beijing appears

---

25 Middle East Media Reporting Initiative, "Military Correspondent Lavrov: For Now, The Disadvantages Of American Bases In The Former Central Asian Soviet Republics Bordering On Afghanistan Outweigh The Benefits," Special Dispatch No. 9583, October 11, 2021. memri.org/reports/military-correspondent-lavrov-now-disadvantages-american-bases-former-central-asian-soviet

26 Anton Kolodyazhnyy, "Taliban delegation to join Moscow talks next week - report." *Reuters*, October 14, 2021. https://www.reuters.com/world/asia-pacific/taliban-delegation-join-moscow-talks-next-week-report-2021-10-14/

to be slowly sliding away from neutrality, and to Xi-formulated "unlimited friendship", trade, and diplomatic support. If China decides to provide direct military assistance with weapons, spare parts, critical components, and even personnel, this would escalate the conflict to a whole new level.

Thus far, Russia has managed its relationship with China deftly, happy to play a junior partner so long as it furthers the Kremlin's geopolitical (anti-Western) interests. But the sustainability of the course will decided on the battlefields of Ukraine.

The Taliban is not a unified, centrally controlled entity, nor does it control Al Qaeda and ISIS-K. A clash on the Tajik-Afghan border may result in a war and draw Russia into a meatgrinder of an unknown duration against its will. Economic competition with China will be fierce, given the scope of the Belt and Road Initiative and China's massive economic potential. That match Russia is doomed to lose.

The mutually beneficial energy security relationship between the Central Asian states and China is in particular a serious obstacle to Russia's regional ambitions, and it remains to be seen how Moscow can counter Beijing, if at all. A quasi-alliance of sorts may be possible, at least in areas where Sino-Russian interests do not clash. This is a short sentence with four qualifiers.

Extremist and terrorist threats emanating from Afghanistan are the most immediate security concerns to Russia in Asia, and thus the top priority of any Russian geopolitical strategist outside of Ukraine.

Should instability and extremism begin to escape Afghan borders, a Russian response – with or without China – will be absolutely necessary. Russia simply cannot maintain its sphere of influence if it cannot protect the basic security needs of Central

Asia, its ability to project power contingent on its perception as a competent security partner and power broker. Should its role in these two capacities come into question, which is entirely possible given the commitments in personnel, weapons systems, and materiel, and budgetary constraints in Ukraine, it would spurn the creation of a new security paradigm and likely see China assume the role that Russia once claimed – hegemon of Central Asia.

Simultaneous engagement in Ukraine, Central Asia and in the Caucasus may be even more unsustainable for Russia. Turkey recently initiated the expansion of the Organization of Turkic States to Russia's dismay, and some interpreted the Kazakhstan CSTO mission as a strong message to Ankara as well. How the Kremlin manages its involvement in Kazakhstan – and whether the ultimate outcome is a net positive or net negative for Russian influence – will be a bellwether for future adventures in the region. At the very least, Russia is left emboldened and more confident post-Kazakhstan -- until the debacle in Ukraine.

As Turkish power and ambition grows and Iran expresses increased interest in the areas to its North-West, Russia is destined to increase its involvement in the Caucasus as well. Thus, Washington's engagements with Central Asia, and especially with Kazakhstan and Uzbekistan because of the looming Chinese and Russian involvement, and with Armenia, Azerbaijan, and Georgia are crucial for the U.S. policy vis-à-vis Russia, Turkey and Iran. It is in the U.S.'s strategic interests to keep an eye on Moscow's gambits in these two crucial geographic regions, and maintain and increase its political and military presence there in the years to come.

Iran's Policy toward the Caucasus and Central Asia

Brenda Shaffer

Much of the analysis on Iranian foreign policy focuses on both Iran's location as a state in the Middle East and its claim that Iran's foreign policy should triumph the rights of Muslims in various locations. However, However, Iran shares a border several states of the South Caucasus and Central Asia and its ties with this region affects Iran's national security and even domestic security, since many of Iran's ethnic minorities share ties with co-ethnics in neighboring states. In addition, Tehran, despite its rhetoric, conducts a realpolitik foreign policy in conflicts such as the Armenia-Azerbaijan conflict and its relationship with Central Asian states.

Many Western policy makers relate to Iran as a Middle East country. However, Iran straddles the Caucasus and Central Asia, sharing over half of its borders with states in the region. Therefore, developments in the region can directly affect Iran's security and core interests. Successful policies toward Iran will take into consideration the significance of its interaction with the Caucasus and Central Asia, and not just the Middle East. Events in the

Caucasus and Central Asia directly affect Iran's security not only as a bordering country, but they also can project onto Iran's domestic political arena and affect the stability of the ruling regime. This is because ethnic groups in Iran share ties with co-ethnic regions – chiefly Azerbaijan and Turkmenistan. Consequently, the chief factors in Iran's policy toward the region are defensive: preventing events in the region from negatively affecting its national security and domestic political arena. While the Iranian regime formally declares that its foreign policy is based on Islamic solidarity, Tehran almost always puts pragmatic concerns above religious fraternity, especially in its close neighborhood. Iran's policy toward the region is guided by realpolitik: In conflicts waging in the region, Tehran sides mostly with non-Muslim countries, Armenia and Russia, versus the Muslim sides. In fact, Iran's closest ally in the region, Armenia, has occupied close to twenty percent of the territory of majority-Shia populated Azerbaijan, which is Iran's main nemesis in the region, despite sharing common Shia faith. Iran focuses its policies in the Caucasus and Central Asia on the state-to-state level with the governments of the region. At the same time, it maintains clandestine ties to representatives of local Islamic and ethnic groups that could serve a lever of influence over the states in the region. For instance, Iran sponsors the Huseynyun brigades, which aim to overthrow the government in the Republic of Azerbaijan and maintain regular television and other media broadcasts from Qom. Tehran models the Huseynyun brigades on other militias it sponsors in the Middle East, such as the Hizballah in Lebanon.[1]

---

1   For more on ethnic politics in Iran and the connection to ties of the ethnic groups with the Republic of Azerbaijan and Turkmenistan, see Brenda Shaffer, *Iran is more than Persia: Ethnic Politics in Iran* Berlin: De Gruyter, 2022. For more on the topic of Iran's pragmatism, see: Brenda Shaffer, "The Islamic Republic of Iran: Is it really?" in Shaffer, *Limits of Culture: Islam and Foreign Policy*, Cambridge, MA: MIT Press, 2006.

Iran prefers, however, to promote its direct ties with the ruling governments in the region and primarily activates these other levers of influence only when it needs a tool to coerce policy change in certain states, or to threaten to destabilize governments that do not conform to Iran's demands. Iran maintains exceptionally large embassies and numbers of diplomats in the states of the region, something that helps facilitate this clandestine infrastructure. This paper will examine the main factors that guide Iran's policy toward the Caucasus and Central Asia.

Main Foreign Policy Factors

Iran's policy toward the region is guided by five main factors: First, Iran's national security. Second, prevention of anti-regime activity of Iran's Azerbaijani and Turkmen minorities. Third, Iran's relations with third parties, chiefly Turkey and Russia. Fourth, Iran's leadership role and integration in regional transit, transportation, and energy trade routes. Fifth and finally, economic benefits.

From day one following the collapse of the USSR, Tehran viewed the independence of the new states in the Caucasus and Central Asia as potentially threatening to its national security. The new post-Soviet states, most of them Muslim-majority, were not viewed as objects of export of Islam or revolution, but rather as potential sources of ethno-nationalism that could project onto Iran's domestic arena. The *Tehran Times* editorial following the Soviet collapse clearly articulated Iran's concern that the new neighboring states could be sources of domestic instability that could affect Iran:

From the point of view in Tehran is the lack of political stability in the newly independent republics. The unstable conditions in those republics could be serious causes of insecurity along the lengthy borders (over 2,000 kilometers) Iran shares with those countries. Already foreign hands can be felt at work in those republics, [e]specially in Azerbaijan and Turkmenistan republics, with the ultimate objective of brewing discord among the Iranian Azerbaijanis and Turkmen by instigating ethnic and nationalistic sentiments.[2]

Iran's foreign policy toward its neighbors in the Caucasus and Central Asia is also linked to domestic issues. More than half of Iran's citizens are of non-Persian origin. Most of Iran's major ethnic minorities share ties with co-ethnics in bordering states: Azerbaijan, Turkmenistan, Turkey, Iraq, and Pakistan. Three of Iran's border regions – with Iraq, Turkey, and Pakistan – are security hotspots with the shared ethnic factor playing a major role. Conflict between Armenia and Azerbaijan at times at spilled over to Iranian territory as well.

Iran's policy toward Afghanistan is also guided by security concerns. Tehran promotes multiple interests in Afghanistan, including the protection and power of the Shia Hazara minority and other allies. In addition, Tehran strives for influence in the Herat region, which it views as part of historic greater Iran. However, its primary goal is preventing developments that could affect its national security, such as increased refugee flows into Iran.

Several regional and global powers are located near or active in the Caucasus and Central Asia. The borders of Iran, Turkey and Russia converge in the Caucasus. Tehran thus strives to maintain influence over the strategic architecture of the Caucasus and aims to limit Russian and especially Turkish military presence in the region and those states' control over major transport infrastructure, especially roads and rail that are close to Iran's border or that Iran

---

2 "Gorbachev's Downfall, and New Concerns in Iran," *Tehran Times*, December 30, 1991.

regularly uses, such as the road to Armenia. That said, Iran does not seek conflict with Russia, and has tended to back down in any cases where their policies conflict in the region. Iran also strives to minimize the influence and presence of Israel[3] and United States in the region.

Competition between the regional powers also spills over at times to their domestic arenas. In recent years, Iran has increased its support for the Kurdish separatist terrorist organization PKK (Kurdistan Workers' Party) that frequently conducts terrorist attacks in Turkey and at the Turkish—Iranian border. In response, Turkey has increased its vocal support for the rights of the Azerbaijani Turks in Iran (close to a third or Iran's population).

Throughout the post-Soviet period, Iran has sought to influence the establishment of regional transit, transportation and energy trade in the Caucasus and Central Asia in a manner that promotes its regional role and would create dependence of the landlocked region on Iran. However, over the years, most of Iran's initiatives in this sphere have been declined.

Iran does not play a major role in energy trade in the region, despite its efforts. The bulk of the major energy export from the region flows to the west from Azerbaijan via Georgia and Turkey to the open sea (Azerbaijan's Baku-Tbilisi-Ceyhan Pipeline and two natural gas export pipelines – the South Caucasus Pipeline and the Southern Gas Corridor; through Russia (Kazakhstan's CPC oil pipeline); or from Central Asia to China (Kazakhstan's

---

3   Some analysts have explained Iran's hostility toward the Republic of Azerbaijan as a response to Baku's close ties with Israel, depicting Iran as being on the defensive in light of the cooperation between Israel and Azerbaijan. The timeline of this claim is simply not correct. Strategic cooperation between Azerbaijan and Israel commenced in 1995/1996. In contrast, Tehran has acted against Azerbaijan from the reestablishment of independence in 1991, long before Baku formed close links with Israel. For more on Iran's policy toward Israel's presence in the region, see Brenda Shaffer, "Israel's role in the second Armenia-Azerbaijan war and its implications for the future," *CACI Analyst*, September 9, 2022. https://www.cacianalyst.org/publications/feature-articles/item/13735-israel's-role-in-the-second-armenia-azerbaijan-war-and-its-implications-for-the-future.html

oil pipeline to China; and Turkmenistan's major natural gas export to China via neighbors in Central Asia, which also transits modest gas export from Kazakhstan and Uzbekistan). Iran's energy trade with the region is limited to natural gas exports to Armenia (in barter exchange for electricity imports from Armenia to Iran); transit of Azerbaijani natural gas to Nakhichevan, Azerbaijan's exclave; limited Iranian gas imports from Turkmenistan⁴ and periodical transit of Turkmenistan's gas exports westward.

While Iran and Russia cooperate in many fields, the states are potential competitors in the field of natural gas export. Russia worked to ensure that Iran was blocked from reaching gas markets in Europe via the Caucasus and challenge Russia's dominance there. In response to Iran establishing gas export to Armenia, Gazprom bought the gas pipeline between the states and imposed a small circumference on it, so that it could not transit significant gas volumes and thus serve as a link to Europe. Iran's involvement in regional gas trade is posed to decline further with the planned establishment of a natural gas pipeline that will link Nakhichevan directly to the Turkish pipeline system and thus eliminate the need for Azerbaijan to supply its exclave through transit through Iran.

Over the years, Iran has used the dispute over Caspian Sea border demarcation as a means to try to block Caspian energy projects or at least impose Iranian inclusion. At times, such as July 2001 when Tehran sent gun boats targeting a BP survey vessel, the demarcation dispute raised tensions between Iran and Azerbaijan. However, in 2018, all the Caspian Sea states signed a demarcation agreement and all, but Iran consider the issue resolved. Despite

---

4   Iran, while sitting on the second largest natural gas reserves in the world, regularly has gas shortages in the domestic market and is actually a net natural gas importer.

signing it, successive Iranian governments have not brought he agreement to the Iranian parliament for ratification.

Trade and Transportation

Iran is interested in playing a major role in the rail and road transportation systems that link Asia and Europe, which transit Central Asia and the Caucasus, as well as serving as an export outlet for trade to and from the landlocked Caspian region. T With the exception of Georgia, all the states of the Caucasus and Central Asia are landlocked.[5] Thus, potential transit states, like Iran, gain influence through serving as the trade outlet for this landlocked region. Through greater volumes of trade and transportation, Tehran aims for commercial benefits, as well as political benefits through deepening integration with Central Asia and the Caucasus and also building these states' dependencies on Iran.

Iran is linked with Central Asia and the Caucasus via the rail and freight Middle Corridor. Thus, both Iran and the greater region share an interest in the prominence of this corridor. In response to the limitations on trade from Russia's Black Sea ports due to the invasion of Ukraine, the prospects of use of the Middle Corridor have grown significantly.

Iran is also linked to the South Caucasus and onward to Russia through the North-South Corridor railway route. This line is not functioning optimally since Iran has not s completed a major section – Rasht to Astara – mandating use of trucks for part of the transit through Iran, thus raising costs and increasing transportation times, lowering the attractiveness of this route.

---

5   For more on how the landlocked geography of the Caucasus and Central Asia affects the region, see Avinoam Idan and Brenda Shaffer "The Foreign Policies of Post-Soviet Landlocked States," *Post-Soviet Affairs*, vol. 27 no. 3, 2011, pp. 241-286.

Iran's trade volumes with the Caucasus and Central Asia are modest despite its proximity to the region. None of the countries of the region are among Iran's top five trade partners. According to Iranian media, Iran's trade with the other Caspian littoral states (excluding Russia) in 2021-2022, stood at approximately US$ 1.2 billion.[6]

Iran's provinces that border the Caspian Sea (Gilan, Mazandaran, Gulestan) are particularly engaged in direct foreign trade with the neighboring states. East Azerbaijan province conducts direct trade also with the Republic of Azerbaijan. This trade line enables the residents of these provinces to interact regularly with the neighboring states and increased trade provides economic benefits to these provinces.

Iran's trade and cooperation with the states of Central Asia and the Caucasus is facilitated by special agreements between Iran and the Eurasian Economic Union (EAE) and the Shanghai Cooperation Council. From October 2019, a preferential trade agreement (PTA) was implemented between Iran and the EAEU members, which allows for lower tariffs on 862 commodities, of which over 500 Iran exports to the EAEU region. Among EAEU members states, Armenia was Iran's second largest export market after Russia.[7] In September 2021, Iran's request for membership in the Shanghai Cooperation Organization (SCO) was approved. The SCO is led by China and members include Russia, Central Asian states, Pakistan, and India. Iran's SCO membership will generate only modest trade and political benefits.

In contrast to its professed Islamic solidarity, during the

---

6   "Iran's Trade With Caspian States Hit $3.4b in Fiscal 2021-22," *Financial Tribune*, May 10, 2022.
7   Vali Kaleji, "Iran and Eurasian Economic Union Negotiations: Upgrading EAEU-Iran Preferential Trade Agreement into a Free Trade Agreement," Russian International Affairs Council, January 24, 2022. https://russiancouncil.ru/en/analytics-and-comments/columns/middle-east-policy/iran-and-eurasian-economic-union-negotiations-upgrading-eaeu-iran-preferential-trade-agreement-into-/.

period of Armenia's occupation of close to twenty percent of neighboring Azerbaijan's territory, Iran engaged in direct trade and cooperation with the Armenian occupation authorities. As part of this cooperation, Iranian and Armenia established a hydropower plant complex and dams on the Araz river near the Khudafarin Bridge, which is on the border between Iran and the previously occupied territories.[8] In addition, over forty Iranian companies operated in Azerbaijan's territories during the three decades of Armenian occupation.[9] As part of this, an Iranian company even conducted restorations of the Govhar aga mosque in Shusha. Iran also shared technology with the Armenian occupation authorities for building underground tunnels that facilitated its illicit trade with Iran and contributed to Armenia's war effort.

The 2020 Armenia-Azerbaijan War

Tehran's policies toward the 2020 Armenia-Azerbaijan War are illustrative of the factors that guide Iranian policy toward the greater region of the Caucasus and Central Asia. Iran's alliance with Armenia illustrates the non-ideological nature of Iranian foreign policy, when there are geopolitical trade-offs for implementing these policies. In the case of the war between Iran's two northern neighbors, the clash between ideology and pragmatic considerations was unmistakable: Christian Armenia had invaded Shiite Azerbaijan, captured close to a fifth percent of its territory, and turned almost a million Azerbaijani Shiites into refugees. Tehran hoped that the devastation and poverty created by the

---

8   After the establishment of the hydropower plant, in 2016 Iran and Azerbaijan signed an agreement formally allowing Iran to use the occupied territories, thus Iran formally recognized of Azerbaijan's sovereignty over the territory.

9   "İşğal zamanı Qarabağda fəaliyyət göstərən İran şirkətləri – Siyahı," Qavqazinfo.az October 11, 2021. (https://qafqazinfo.az/news/detail/isgal-zamani-qarabagda-fealiyyet-gosteren-iran-sirketleri-siyahi-339172.)

war and occupation in Azerbaijan in the early years of the conflict would serve the Iranian regime's goal of limiting ties between its Azerbaijani minority and the new Republic of Azerbaijan. As part of this policy, Tehran supported Yerevan in its wars with Azerbaijan and has continued close security cooperation with Armenia.

Tehran acknowledges that its stance toward the conflict is forged by its national security interests and especially its domestic security concern due to its Azerbaijani minority. Mahmoud Va'ezi, who served as Deputy Foreign Minister of Iran, responsible for the former Soviet region during the first war in the early 1990s, pointed to internal considerations as one of Iran's major factors in its policy toward the Karabakh conflict:

> Iran was in the neighborhood of the environment of
> the conflict. Karabakh is situated only 40 km distance
> from its borders. At that time, this possibility raised
> that the boundaries of conflict extended to the beyond
> of Karabakh. Since then, Iran's consideration was
> based on security perceptions. [...] Iran could not be
> indifferent to the developments occurring along its
> borders, security changes of the borders and their
> impact on Iran's internal developments.[10]

Iran has been an active player in the Armenia- Azerbaijan conflict, supporting Armenia in both the First (1992-94) and the Second Armenia-Azerbaijan War in 2020. During both wars, Iran served as the main channel of supplies to Armenia. In the 2020 war, Iran's involvement in the conflict reached a new height,

---

10 Mahmud Va'ezi in Interfax (in English), March 25, 1992 (FBIS-SOV-92-059). See, also, Tehran Times, March 10, 1992, p. 2 for reference to the internal Azerbaijan and Armenian factor as affecting its suitability to mediate in the conflict.

with Iranian forces crossing the border into Azerbaijan's territory several times, where they disrupted the battlefield advances of the Azerbaijani forces. When Azerbaijan's forces reached the province of Zangilan, which borders Iran, and were engaged in serious battles with Armenia, Iranian forces crossed the border into Azerbaijan on October 17, 2020, and placed large concrete blocks on the road in a section in Jabrayil region, close to Zangilan, cutting the Azerbaijani forces in Zangilan from supplies and reinforcements.[11]

In addition, during the 2020 war, Iranian forces also crossed several times into Nakhichevan, Azerbaijan's exclave that borders Iran.[12] Tehran also blocked communications of the Azerbaijani forces at times during the war and provided Armenia with information on Azerbaijani troop movements in the provinces that border Iran. Iran had access to information on Azerbaijani troop movements since Iranian intelligence units were able to intercept communications of Azerbaijani troops as well as to observe their movements.[13]

Russia supplied Armenia during the war both via flights that overflew Iran and also via land shipments from Iran's Anzali port on the Caspian Sea. This indicates the coordination between Russia, Iran and Armenia on security and military matters.

Iran's regional position and security has weakened as a result of the 2020 war. The security architecture that emerged in the South Caucasus following the 2020 war between Armenia and

---

11 "How Iran invaded Azerbaijan during 44-Day War in 2020," Contreras Report YouTube, October 10, 2021. Accessed at: https://www.youtube.com/watch?v=iuzJbnI12xw.

12 Author's interviews, October 2020.

13 Author's interviews, September 2021; "How Iran invaded Azerbaijan during 44-Day War in 2020," Contreras Report YouTube, October 10, 2021. Accessed at: https://www.youtube.com/watch?v=i-uzJbnI12xw; "Иран вторгся в Азербайджан: сенсационные подробности 44-дневной войны," Caliber, October 9, 2021. Accessed at: https://caliber.az/ru/post/28990/.

Azerbaijan led to significant changes for the region's three main powers: Russia and Turkey gained increased power in the region, while Iran's leverage in the region declined. The war outcomes also strengthened domestic challenges from Iran's large ethnic Azerbaijani community, which opposed Tehran's support for Armenia in the war. Iran's support for Armenia in the 2020 war catalyzed waves of anti-regime protests against the ruling regime among the ethnic Azerbaijanis in Iran.

Iran acts to prevent resolution of the conflict between Armenia and Azerbaijan. Accordingly, since the November 2020 ceasefire, Iran has sent arms to Armenia, and IRGC officers and trainers to the Armenian population in Karabakh (areas under control of the Russian peacekeepers). Tehran especially wants to prevent the opening of the Zangezur Corridor which would eliminate Turkish reliance on Iran for transit and Azerbaijan's dependence on Iran for connection to its exclave Nakhichivan. Tehran also wants to prevent Turkish and Russian presence in close proximity to its border with Armenia and keep open its illicit trade route with Armenia.

Among all the states of the region, Iran enjoys the deepest cooperation with Armenia, and the most conflictual relations with the Republic of Azerbaijan. In late 2022 and early 2023, ties between Baku and Tehran deteriorated to an unprecedented level, with Azerbaijan's President Ilham Aliyev describing relations between Azerbaijan and Iran as "at the lowest level ever," and that in Iran, "terror is organized on a governmental level." These statements follow Iranian government sponsored terrorist attack on the Azerbaijani embassy in Tehran (January 27, 2023) and an assassination attempt (March 28, 2023) on an Azerbaijani member of parliament in Baku.

Conclusions

Many assume that religious based ideology plays a major role in Iran's foreign policy. As this discussion of Iran's policy toward the neighboring states in Central Asia and the Caucasus, the Islamic Republic of Iran could be the posterchild for realpolitik. Iran's primary concern in its interaction with the region is promotion of its national security. Tehran is especially prevention of developments in the region from projecting onto its domestic political arena, since over a third of the population of Iran shares co-ethnic ties with the peoples in Central Asia and the Caucasus. Iran's policies toward neighboring states are much more practical and cautious than those in non-bordering regions, where it can employ ideological rhetoric with few consequences.

Iran and its neighbors in Central Asia and the Caucasus use a high degree of policy compartmentalization in order to simultaneously derive benefit and prevent open conflict. Iran for instance, can cooperate with Azerbaijan on transportation and energy projects, while at the same time render military support to Armenia and sponsor forces aimed at changing the form of government in the Republic of Azerbaijan. The states of the region welcome Iran into regional transportation and economic projects, while at the same time are very cautious about its activity in their domestic arenas.

Washington and Brussels need to further integrate developments and options on Iran's northern borders with its Iran policies. The U.S. and Europe tend to view Iran through the lens of the Middle East. Institutionally, Iran is analyzed primarily as part of the Middle East. In U.S. Department of State and relevant divisions in the American Department of Defense as well as most European state institutions, Iran is analyzed, and policy set within divisions dealing with the Middle East. In contrast, the bordering regions of Central Asia and the Caucasus are generally part of Europe divisions (the Caucasus) and Asia divisions (Central Asia). Thus, despite the fact that Iran borders both regions, and as seen in this paper, interacts intensively, comprehensive policy options toward Iran are often lost.

The Dawn of Turan: Eurasian Opportunity and Challenge for Turkey

Halil Karaveli

Turkey is eager to exploit the opportunity to enhance its influence among the Turkic peoples of Central Asia and sees the "emergence of a new geostrategic force in the heart of Eurasia." But it wants to avoid provoking a reaction from Russia, preferring to advance pan-Turkism without the grandiose rhetoric of the 1990s, and professing a faith in Eurasian multilateralism that in appearance defers to Russia. Yet this may change. Ultimately, how assertive Turkey will become in Central Asia depends on how wounded Russia will emerge from the Ukraine war.

The rediscovery, more than a century ago, of Central Asia, also known as Turkestan, provided the new nation of Turkey with a foundational identity. In fact, the Ottomans had sought to maintain their relationship with Turkestan. In the 16th century, the empire established a western-eastern axis with the Uzbek khanates against the common enemy, Safavid Persia. The Ottomans provided the Uzbeks with military support. Ottoman admiral Seydi Ali Reis, on return from India and battles against the Portuguese in the Indian Ocean, took the way over Central Asia; in his memoirs he related how the Janissaries that had been sent to the Uzbeks had distinguished themselves. Uzbek emissaries to Constantinople pleaded for a continuation of the military cooperation, but the Ottoman interest remained limited to times of war with Persia. In any case, the Russian advance into the Caucasus severed the Ottoman link to Central Asia. It was not until three hundred years later that Ottoman military officers reappeared in Central Asia, this time to counter Russia. The Ottomans took Yakup Beg and his short-lived East Turkestan state under their wings. In the 1870s, Ottoman military instructors were sent to his service. But the Ottomans also saw Central Asia as the solution to their own existential crisis.

The Dream of Turan

As the Ottoman Empire disintegrated, the historical heartland of the empire, the Balkans – from where most of its elite hailed – was irrevocably lost. The intellectual and political elite – dominated by ethnic Macedonians, Albanians, and Bosnians – in its existential agony turned its gaze toward the east, discovering or rather inventing a new, imperial-national allegiance for itself. Turkestan was the heart of a new-old Turkish homeland, Turan, which spanned Eurasia from Crimea and Kazan, birthplaces of pan-Turkism, to China. The Caucasus was its gateway. "The fatherland was Turan, not the Ottoman Empire," wrote Şevket Süreyya Aydemir, a leading intellectual during the early years of the Turkish republic. Aydemir described how as a young student he, like many others in his generation at the beginning of the 20th century, was swept along by the allure of Turan, which was so much more expansive than the crumbling Ottoman state. "The Turkish nation did not begin with the Ottoman state," adolescents like Aydemir were taught, with the implication that neither was it destined to disappear with the Ottomans.

The dream of Turan as an empire of substitution nonetheless proved short-lived. Mustafa Kemal Atatürk, always the political realist, shut the door to imperial adventures, concentrating on building a smaller but secure nation-state in Anatolia. Yet Atatürk the intellectual never lost sight of Central Asia, the cradle – according to him, not only of the Turkish nation and of its forerunners in Anatolia like the Hittites, but of civilization. His rival, the adventurist former Ottoman war minister Enver Pasha nevertheless pursued the dream of Turan to its bitter end: undeterred by the Ottoman failure to expel Russia from the Caucasus, he charged on toward Central Asia, meeting his death in Tajikistan 1922 in a Red Army ambush. The idea of Turan was briefly revived during the Second World War, when for a while it seemed that Nazi Germany was going to defeat the Soviet Union, opening up a new possibility for Turkey to link up with Turan. That moment arrived when the Soviet empire disintegrated 1991, and it was fitting that Turkey became the first country to recognize the independence of Azerbaijan and the Central Asian states.

"Having rejected Mecca, and being rejected by Brussels, Turkey seized the opportunity opened up by the dissolution of the Soviet Union to turn toward Tashkent," wrote Samuel Huntington.[14] President Turgut Özal and his successor Süleyman Demirel held out the vision of a community of Turkic peoples stretching "from the Adriatic to the Wall of China." Yet as Huntington

---

14 Samuel P. Huntington, "The Clash of Civilizations?" *Foreign Affairs*, vol. 72 no. 3, 1993, p. 42.

pointed out, this was not merely a romantic dream but it also spoke of a desire to counter Iran and Saudi Arabia from expanding their influence and promoting Islamic radicalism in the region. And furthermore, Turkey hoped to contain the resurgence of Russian influence. But ultimately it was not Tashkent but Brussels that beckoned for Ankara: at the end of the day, its opening to Central Asia was intended to bolster Turkey's bid for EU membership, by demonstrating that Turkey could serve as a bridge between the West and former Soviet lands to the east, and be an antidote to religious radicalism there. Today, Turkish analysts agree that the 1990s was a "romantic" phase during which Turkey both overestimated its own resources and underestimated Russia's staying power in a region with which it in fact had little if any familiarity. Once again, the dream of Turan had proved to be a mirage.

Yet it was not only Russia's reassertion of its influence, its application of pressure and inducements that pushed Central Asia to the background in Turkish foreign policy. While the Central Asians were attentive to Russia and generally swung back to their former imperial master, stressing the need for "balanced" relationships, Turkey itself increasingly turned its attention to the West – in its case Brussels – obtaining candidate status with the EU 1999. And after the Islamic conservative Justice and Development Party (AKP) rose to power 2002, Turkey followed a dual track, pursuing first the EU membership goal and later the role of Sunni leadership in the Middle East. Both goals were to prove elusive, and with the latter abandoned altogether, the conclusion seems foregone that Turkey now seeks to compensate by seeking influence and economic gains in the Caucasus and in Central Asia. The "Islamic card and talk of Muslim unity no longer work" and are being replaced by Turkish nationalism, remarks Hüseyin Bağcı, head of Ankara-based Foreign Policy Institute.[15]

The Ascent of Nationalism in the Turkish State

Indeed, in terms of ideology Turkey's pivot to Central Asia is underpinned by the ascent of nationalists in the state establishment. Obviously, these have always been preeminent in the Turkish state, but their grip has become even stronger since President Recep Tayyip Erdoğan in 2015 turned to the far-right Nationalist Movement Party (MHP) and its leader Devlet Bahçeli as an ally. Fresh ülkücü cadres (right-wing nationalists) have filled the void after the Islamist Gülenists, on whom Erdoğan first relied to exercise power – but who were purged from the state after their 2016 attempt to overthrow Erdoğan. Erdoğan also relies on *ulusalcı* (left-wing nationalist) cadres that are particularly strong in the military. Both ülkücü and *ulusalcı* nationalists have an emotional attachment to Turkic unity and to Central Asia as the cradle of Turkish culture and civilization. Yet in contrast to the 1990s when pan-Turkic emotions ran high, Turkish officals and analysts today make a point of avoiding romanticism and illusions; they point out that Turkic unity is still hampered by important divisions between the Turkic states in Central Asia, that very little headway has until recently been made in terms of political cooperation and above all that the potential for economic cooperation, great as it is, nonetheless remains seriously underdeveloped. It is still Russia and of course China that enjoy the upper hand in Central Asia. A case in point is the customs union that Russia has established within the Eurasian Economic Union with Kazakhstan, Kyrgyzstan,

---

15 Stefan Hedlund, "Turkey's Push for Greater Influence in Central Asia," GIS Reports, April 9, 2021. (https://www.gisreportsonline.com/r/turkey-central-asia/)

Belarus and Armenia and which has put Turkey in an even more disadvantaged position. As Cengiz Buyar, historian at the Kyrgyz-Turkish Manas University remarks, Turkey has lost market shares in to Russia in these countries after increases of up to forty percent in customs duties.[16] Developing trade is Turkey's highest priority. Turkish foreign minister Mevlüt Cavuşoğlu emphasizes that the opportunity that the Middle Corridor offers must be used to remove the obstacles to transportation and trade.[17]

The gateway to Central Asia is Azerbaijan, the Turkic country with which Turkey has developed the deepest relationship. Ultimately, it is Azerbaijan's victory in the Second Nagorno-Karabakh war 2020 that makes a Turkish new opening to Central Asia viable in the first place with the projected Nakhichevan-Zangezur corridor. Indeed, Turkey's relationship with Azerbaijan is not only the key to Central Asia; it also provides a model for how Turkey's future relations with the Turkic states of Central Asia may evolve when mutual economic interests and security needs of the latter converge to create a Turkic cooperative synergy. While the countries of Turan offer Turkey economic opportunities, Turkey has in turn demonstrated that it has the capacity to attend to their security needs. Moreover, the dynamic of the Turkish-Azerbaijani relationship illustrates how other Turkic countries' needs and empowerment affect Turkey's own foreign policy. A particularly telling case in point was when Turkey's courting of Armenia in 2008-10, which clashed with the interests of Azerbaijan, was subsequently abandoned. Indeed, the impact that the rise of Azerbaijan as a Turkic mid-size power has had on Turkey's foreign policy

---

16 Cengiz Buyar, "Yükselen bir değer olarak Asya ve Türkiye nin rolü," *Anadolu Ajansı*, April 14, 2021.

17 "Mevlut Cavusoglu: "Geopolitical problems create new opportunities for the Middle Corridor," Azreport.az, August 2, 2022. (https://report.az/en/infrastructure/mevlut-cavusoglu-geopolitical-prob-lems-create-new-opportunities-for-the-middle-corridor/)

identity should not be underestimated. Just as the notion of Turkic unity did not originate in Ottoman Turkey but in Tsarist Russia (in Kazan, Crimea and Azerbaijan,) similarly the political-intellectual groundwork for Turkic cooperation, into which Turkey is effectively being pulled, has been laid outside Turkey. Indeed, the Turks do not pretend otherwise; they recognize Nursultan Nazarbayev as the "father of Turkic unity" as well as the crucial role played by Heydar Aliyev, who coined "one nation, two states" as the foundational principle of the relationship between Azerbaijan and Turkey. Today, this principle has been expanded to "one nation, two states acting as one state," demonstrated during the Second Karabakh war and subsequently enshrined in the strategic alliance of Azerbaijan and Turkey.

Similarly, the strategic partnership between Kazakhstan and Turkey, which was concluded in 2022, speaks of the deepening relationship between the two states. While Kazakh-Turkish relations have for long remained strikingly underdeveloped in terms of trade and investments, there is now a strong commitment to develop the political-strategic dimension, which has economic implications, with the co-production of drones.

Former president Nursultan Nazarbayev is held in particular esteem in Turkey for two reasons. First, the initiative that Nazarbayev took in 2015 to defuse the crisis between Russia and Turkey that followed on Turkey's downing of a Russian fighter jet on the Turkish-Syrian border is recognized as having been crucial in averting a threatening escalation.[18] Second, Nazarbayev's demonstration of solidarity with the Turkish government after the

---

18 See Svante E. Cornell and S. Frederick Starr, *Kazakhstan's Role in International Mediation under First President Nursultan Nazarbayev*, Silk Road Paper, Central Asia-Caucasus Institute & Silk Road Studies Program, November 2020. (https://silkroadstudies.org/publications/silkroad-papers-and-monographs/item/13397)

2016 coup attempt – when Turkey's Western allies conspicuously withheld any such expressions of solidarity – earned Ankara's lasting gratitude.

Turkey attaches a particular value to developing its relationship with Uzbekistan, which was deep-frozen during the presidency of Islam Karimov, who distrusted Turkey ideologically. This is the case not least because of the central place that Uzbekistan occupies in the history of Turkic civilization. Turkey anticipates that the relationship is set to evolve further with the realization of the middle corridor, which will offer Uzbekistan a new route to Western markets. Meanwhile, Uzbekistan and Kyrgyzstan are also, alongside Kazakhstan, becoming markets for Turkish military technology. Indeed, the military dimension in Turkey's commitment to Central Asia at a time of great geopolitical upheaval in Eurasia has potentially far-reaching implications for Turkey's Eurasian strategy and orientations. It raises the question whether and to what extent Turkey can reconcile its advances and initiatives in Central Asia with its overarching Eurasian strategy.

Reconciling Turkish Interests with Russia Relations

As the academic Mehmet Yüce euphemistically notes in a recent report from the Turkish pro-government think-tank SETA, Russia's "new foreign policy that is being displayed in Ukraine" is one reason that has impelled Kazakhstan to seek strategic partnership and deeper relations with Turkey.[19] However, its failure in Central Asia in the 1990s taught Turkey not to disregard Russia. With this failure in mind, success in the region is deemed possible only

---

19 Mehmet Yüce, *Türkiye'nin Türk Devletleri Teşkilatı Üyeleriyle İkili İlişkileri*, SETA, 2022, p. 16. (https://www.setav.org/rapor-turkiyenin-turk-devletleri-teskilati-uyeleriyle-ikili-iliskileri/)

with Moscow's tacit acquiescence. This was mostly true before the Ukraine war, which changed balances and perceptions on how much one must defer to Moscow. But Burhanettin Duran, director of SETA and an advisor to President Erdoğan, still argues that "Turkey and Azerbaijan stand to benefit from pursuing a balanced policy in the competition between the West and Russia."[20] Russia's stance during the Second Karabakh war represented an "interesting example of the harmony between the Turkish and Russian worlds," states Fırat Purtaş, the author of another recent report from SETA.[21] Ankara, writes Purtaş, "has not pursued a strategy in its relations with the Turkic states that challenges Moscow." This is manifestly not accurate when it comes to Azerbaijan. For Turkey to militarily insert itself in the Caucasus definitely challenged Moscow, just as it did in Syria and Libya, but it did so in a way that would offer Moscow a way to accept Turkey's presence. In this context, the fact that Turkey, while a member of NATO, is overtly acting in a way that opposes Western hegemony is the major change that allows Moscow to accept, though reluctantly, a Turkish presence. Today, Turkish presence in the Caucasus or Central Asia is not an extension of Western presence, and this is what makes it acceptable to Russia – which is also why Russia does not want to worsen its relationship with Ankara even though it encroaches on Russian interests.

Turkish pro-government academics are eager to reassure that Turkey "is sensitive to Russia's interests" and that it "acts in harmony with the multi-dimensional foreign policy strategies of the Turkic states." This is an inversion of what transpired in the 1990s: what then proved to be an insurmountable obstacle

---

20 Burhanettin Duran, "Yeni Jeopolitikte Ankara ve Bakü'nün imkânları," *Sabah*, October 21, 2022.

21 Fırat Purtaş, Krizleri Fırsata Dönüştüren İş Birliği: Türk Devletleri Teşkilatı, SETA, 2022, p. 21. (Krizleri Fırsata Dönüştüren İş Birliği: Türk Devletleri)

to Turkey's ambitions – the fact that the Central Asian states privileged maintaining their close relations with Russia – is now viewed as something that on the contrary makes it possible for Turkey to become involved in Central Asia, and to reconcile its Turkic and larger Eurasian ambitions. The academic Yüce notes that the sensitive military, political and economic projects that are envisioned within the framework of the Organization of Turkic States "have the potential to draw the attention or provoke the reaction of third parties."[22] He suggests that the reactions of third parties will be mitigated if these projects are instead launched bi- or trilaterally among the Turkic states, and appropriated by the Organization of Turkic states at a later stage.

What has fundamentally changed since the 1990s is that the nationalist Turkish state establishment has increasingly come to see Russia as a balancing factor against the West, if not as a geopolitical partner. While it may still be a rival – in Eurasia, the Middle East and North Africa – Russia is no longer seen as an enemy. Since the end of the Cold War, the idea of a strategic realignment has gained considerable traction among the Turkish state elite. The secularist-progressive nationalists in particular have since the early 2000s seen Russia as a partner in resisting Western global hegemony. The right-wing nationalists on the other hand have traditionally feared and resented Russia. But the perception of a manifest hostility of the United States toward Turkey – with the U.S. supporting the Kurdish militants in Syria that are affili-ated with the Kurdistan Workers' Party, (PKK) which has waged an insurgency against Turkey since 1984 – has changed the geo-political perceptions also of the right-wing nationalists. But under

---

22 Mehmet Yüce, *Türkiye'nin Türk Devletleri Teşkilatı Üyeleriyle İkili İlişkileri*, SETA, 2022, p. 34. (https://www.setav.org/rapor-turkiyenin-turk-devletleri-teskilati-uyeleriyle-ikili-iliskileri/)

the shadow of a war in Ukraine to which no end is in sight, "balancing" Russian interests against Central Asian interests that no longer by definition align with those of Russia, is an unexpected, and likely difficult, challenge for Turkey.

Having acted on the assumption that its increased involvement in Central Asia could and should be carried out in harmony with Russia, the fact that Russia's "big brother attitude" has become cause for growing concern for the Turkic states – in particular for Kazakhstan – is vexing for Turkey. The analyses of pro-government Turkish academics suggests that Turkey, although it will help bolster the defenses of the Central Asian states, does not envision pan-Turkic political cooperation taking on a pro-Western, and certainly not anti-Russian role. "The Turkic states defend multi-polarity against the global hegemony of the United States, give priority to strengthening their own sovereignties and seek to prevent global and regional conflicts from spreading to them," writes the academic Fırat Purtaş of SETA. But this makes no sense – Western hegemony is not an issue for these states, who want more, not less, western presence to counterbalance Russia and China. Nonetheless, this line of reasoning does suggest that the ideologues of the Turkish regime perceive Turkey's relationship to Central Asia in the same light as its relationship with Russia: as a strategic diversification, an antidote to Western hegemony. This, of course, represents a dramatic shift compared to the 1990s, when Turkey promoted the idea of itself as Central Asia's bridge to the West.

Conclusion

Meanwhile, there is a keen awareness that the strategic environment of the Central Asian states is fraught with dangers that make a closer Turkic cooperation – and importantly, equidistance to the rival great powers – imperative. Listing the threats to Central Asia's stability, Purtaş observes that "Russia's aggressive policies, the return of the Taliban to power in Afghanistan, Iran's expansionist Shiite geopolitics, China's increasing influence in also the western part of Turkestan after Eastern Turkestan and the ambition of the United States to turn the Turkic world into a new frontline in the confrontation with Russia and China impel the member states of the Organization of Turkic States to closer political and security cooperation." Inevitably, this will require a serious and lasting commitment to Central Asia by Turkey.

Turkey is eager to exploit the opportunity to enhance its influence among the Turkic peoples of Central Asia, and sees the "emergence of a new geostrategic force in the heart of Eurasia." But it wants to avoid provoking a reaction from Russia, preferring to advance pan-Turkism without the grandiose rhetoric of the 1990s, and professing a faith in Eurasian multilateralism that in appearance defers to Russia. Yet this may change. Ultimately, how assertive Turkey will become in Central Asia depends on how wounded Russia will emerge from the Ukraine war.

The EU'S Growing Presence in Central Asia and the Caucasus

Svante E. Cornell

The EU has taken an incrementally greater interest in Central Asia and the Caucasus over time. While it has had a tendency to address the region on the basis of its own logic of enlargement, in recent years, as the EU is transitioning into a role that fits in a new geopolitically dominated world, its involvement in security issues has grown considerably. The EU has begun to interact with the region's states at the highest levels, a process accelerated by the Russian invasion of Ukraine.

EU Engagement Since Independence

The EU engagement with Central Asia and the Caucasus was slow to take off, not least because the EU itself was not, in the 1990s, an actor with its own foreign and security policy. The EU did, however, have economic and transport questions in mind from an early time. Already in 1992, Brussels launched the idea of a Transport Corridor linking Europe across the Caucasus to Asia, known as TRACECA. While TRACECA did not live up to the grandiose ideas at the time, it was a visionary initiative that has gradually been infused with more meaning and substance.

During the 2000s, as the EU embarked on its enlargement into Central and Eastern Europe, it also began to take a greater interest in the Caucasus and Central Asia. The Caucasus was formally included in the European Neighborhood Policy in 2004, and three years later the first EU Strategy for Central Asia was formally presented. Already from this time, the EU drew a sharp distinction between the two: the Caucasus was – albeit reluctantly – accepted as a part of Europe, not least as the three states had already become members of the Council of Europe. As a result, the EU saw the South Caucasus through the prism of its relations with European non-members in the European Neighborhood Policy – states where it sought to develop EU standards, while being very clear that no perspective of membership would be imminent. Thus, the EU lacked a major carrot in the region aside from financial and technical assistance. As for Central Asia, the region was viewed as a purely foreign, non-European region, with which the EU would strive to develop relations as well as engage in foreign aid.

The 2008 Russian invasion of Georgia led the EU to shift its approach to the South Caucasus. It launched the Eastern Partnership in 2009, an instrument that sought greater integration with Ukraine, Moldova, Belarus, and the three states of the Caucasus. The program initially suffered from a one-size-fits-all approach, which did not differentiate between the three states that sought EU membership – Georgia, Moldova and Ukraine – and the others, who did not. It also suffered from the continued unwillingness to grant any notion of a future candidate status to countries that desired it.

Recent Changes in EU Policy and Priorities

The fundamental division between EU approaches to the South Caucasus and Central Asia remains, although it has been softened considerably by the EU's implicit acceptance that a one-size-fits-all approach did not work. As a result, the EU concluded Association Agreements, coupled with Deep and Comprehensive Free Trade Agreements, with countries that sought deeper European integration. While it initially had expected all countries in the Eastern Partnership to do so, the EU was forced to reassess after it became clear that Azerbaijan was not interested, and Armenia was not permitted by Russia to conclude such agreements. Meanwhile, the EU understood the value of Kazakhstan, and signed an Enhanced Partnership and Cooperation Agreement with that country in 2015. After Armenia was blocked from concluding an Association Agreement, the EU instead concluded a Comprehensive and Enhanced Partnership Agreement with Armenia in 2021. While this agreement goes further than the one it signed with Kazakhstan, it is more a difference of degree than of kind – indicating that the deep distinction between EU approaches to countries on either side of the Caspian is being diluted. As the EU gets increasingly interested in security and conflict issues, and not solely in economic and social ones, furthermore, its approach to the region is becoming more strategic.

The launch of a new EU strategy toward Central Asia in 2019 was a major milestone. What started as a roadmap for foreign assistance in the 2000s over time morphed into a complex document seeking to balance a wide array of interests, ranging from the promotion of trade and energy ties to enhanced dialogue in security matters and promotion of regional cooperation as well as a focus on human rights and good governance.

From relatively modest beginnings two decades ago, the EU devoted considerable attention and resources to its relationship with Central Asia – with a very organized approach, involving the production of concrete strategies, reviews of these strategies, and European Council conclusions on the region on a bi-yearly basis. The EU also launched in the 2000s a mechanism of consultation with Central Asian leaders, normally held at the level of foreign ministers. This process allowed the EU and Central Asian leaders, who now met on a bi-yearly basis, to develop closer ties – something that happened in particular during the tenure of Federica Mogherini as EU foreign policy czar. Following the Russian invasion of Ukraine, the EU responded to the growing vulnerability of Central Asian states by raising the level of its dialogue to the presidential level. Both in fall 2022 and summer 2023, EU Council President Charles Michel traveled to Central Asia to meet with his regional counterparts.

The EU has similarly taken a greater interest in matters in the South Caucasus. Here, both Michel and von der Leyen have been directly involved. Michel took a direct role in the turmoil in Georgia. In April 2021, Michel mediated an agreement between the Georgian government and opposition to reduce polarization in the country, end the opposition boycott of parliament, and implement electoral and political reforms. Unfortunately, the government left the agreement in July the same year, and as is now well known, continued on the path of polarization while turning increasingly away from Georgia's Euro-Atlantic orientation. Michel also in 2021 got directly involved in efforts to promote a lasting peace agreement between Armenia and Azerbaijan, hosting the leaders of the two countries on several occasions. His efforts were impeded by French President Emanuel Macron imposing himself into the process, but nevertheless, the EU unexpectedly filled a void that appeared with the second Karabakh war. As for Von der Leyen, in July 2022 she traveled to Baku and concluded a Strategic Partnership in the field of Energy with Azerbaijan, which included the doubling of Azerbaijani natural gas supplies to the EU.

The Russian invasion of Ukraine also led the EU to shift its approach to the Eastern partnership countries that desired further EU integration. In a historic decision, it offered a European perspective – i.e. membership perspective – to Georgia, Moldova and Ukraine in the summer of 2022. While the latter two countries were offered formal candidate status, Georgia was not, on account of its political backsliding, and instead handed a list of areas in which the country needed improvement in order to be considered a formal candidate.

EU's Perception of Processes in the Region

The EU has divided countries outside the EU into different categories, which guide every aspect of the EU's relationship with a state. One consists of candidate states, which aspire to membership. The second is European countries that are in one form or another associated with the EU. The fourth is all others, which are partners to the EU. Central Asian states fall in the latter category, and in the South Caucasus, so do Armenia and Azerbaijan, at least until such date as they would be ready to sign an Association Agreement. As for Georgia, it has been declared potentially eligible for candidate status, a major shift in EU policy. Ironically, this shift came just as Georgia was distancing itself from the EU under the shadow rule of business tycoon Bidzina Ivanishvili.

However, the EU's approach to Central Asia and the

Caucasus has evolved over time. Geographically, the EU's tendency to distinguish sharply between the South Caucasus and Central Asia has attenuated over time, as the EU has been forced by events to approach the region, and the world as a whole, more strategically. Concretely, the EU's own interests in expanding trade and transport, importing energy to replace Russian natural gas, and countering Russian imperialism have contributed to a perspective that appreciates the inter-connection between the two parts of the region.

In this sense, the EU perspective on the region differs from the United States. The U.S. presence in Afghanistan for two decades affected – and somewhat distorted – its approach to Central Asia and the Caucasus. Paradoxically, in spite of the U.S. using the east-west corridor to transport materiel and troops to Afghanistan, its Afghanistan-centric approach led it to adopt a north-south logic to the region's economic development – as indicated in the 2012 launch of the "New Silk Road" initiative, through a speech by Secretary of State Hillary Clinton in Mumbai that did not mention the South Caucasus. By contrast, the EU's interest in the region's energy resources and in continental trade across Central Asia to China has ensured that the EU has continued to remain focused on the east-west corridor.

Conceptually, there has been a clear shift in the EU approach to the region. From an approach that viewed the region as a distant partner, and the EU mainly as a provider of assistance, events in the past several years have led Brussels to take a more strongly interests-based approach to Central Asia and the Caucasus. This has also led to a shift in the EU's approach to political development in the region. In the past, as in the United States, the EU had a strongly normative approach to many countries in Central

Asia and the Caucasus, with the promotion of human rights and democracy central to the EU's approach. Thus, the EU in 2010-2011 unveiled the principle it called "more for more" within the European Neighborhood Policy. This principle implied that the EU "will develop stronger partnerships with those neighbours that make more progress towards democratic reform."

However, more recently the EU appears to have departed from this principle, not least because of the backtracking seen in countries where the EU tried to apply this principle – such as Georgia and Moldova. Moldova's constitutional crisis in 2019 involved a pro-Russian socialist president and a nominally pro-Western oligarch who subsequently fled the country and faced charges of fraud and abuse of office; Georgia's backtracking has already been mentioned. Along with the emergence of gradual reform processes being launched in Kazakhstan, Uzbekistan and Azerbaijan – and the rapidly deteriorating security situation in eastern Europe – the EU appears to have shifted its approach to the region. As a result, EU institutions and leaders have upgraded their relations with countries that are less interested in European integration, but partners to the EU in security and energy matters.

This shifting approach was visible in the 2019 EU Central Asia strategy, which adopted a policy of engagement with the region's largely authoritarian regimes, contrasting with the more-for-more approach adopted earlier for countries further west. This in turn generated criticism from special interest groups focused on democracy promotion; similarly, a considerable portion of the think tank and academic literature on EU policy in Central Asia has criticized the EU's shift. Still, it has rapidly yielded results, as the EU's footprint in Central Asia and the Caucasus has increased as the EU has adopted a more pragmatic approach to the region.

EU Priorities

The EU's priorities in the region are undergoing a shift both in terms of topical areas and countries of focus. In the past, the EU was focused mainly on economic issues and assistance to the countries of Central Asia, and on incorporating the South Caucasus into the European Neighborhood Policy, implying a strong focus on internal regulatory affairs in these countries. Over time, this has shifted. The EU remains a leading donor to the region – in fact, with over one billion Euros in assistance in 2014-20, the EU is the largest foreign donor in Central Asia.[1] But the EU's approach has broadened. As mentioned, the EU has responded to crises in the region of various kinds.

An important starting point was the EU reaction to the Russian invasion of Georgia. While it was French President Nicolas Sarkozy who negotiated the cease-fire, he did so on behalf of the EU as France held the rotating presidency of the Union. In October 2008, the EU deployed the EU Monitoring Mission in Georgia (EUMM), a mission of unarmed observers operating under the EU Common Foreign and Security Policy. Charles Michel's initiative to mediate in Georgian politics, and his efforts to achieve a peace deal between Armenia and Azerbaijan, are further indication of the EU's shift into the political and security-related domain.

A concomitant shift has happened in terms of countries of interest. Following the 2003 Rose Revolution in Georgia, much of the EU's interest in the South Caucasus was directed at that country. In the interim, there has also been interest in Armenia, driven in particular by France's relationship with that country

---

1   European External Action Service, "The EU Development Priorities in Central Asia," March 16, 2022. (https://www.eeas.europa.eu/eeas/eu-development-priorities-central-asia_en)

and Yerevan's abortive interest in signing an Association Agreement. Over time, however, the EU has expanded relations also with Azerbaijan, at par with the EU's growing interest in energy diplomacy and Trans-Caspian transportation.

In Central Asia, the EU has consistently had a priority relationship with Kazakhstan, given the economic attractiveness of that country to European investors, its potential to serve as a transit corridor, and its sheer size. In parallel, however, the EU has expanded its outreach to Uzbekistan. In July 2022, the two sides completed negotiations on an Enhanced Partnership and Cooperation Agreement. In 2023, news reports suggested the EU and Kyrgyzstan may sign a similar agreement before the end of the year.

The EU and Other Powers

The EU's approach to Central Asia and the Caucasus has been largely disconnected from other powers. Its most obvious potential partner is the United States, whose interests in the region largely align with the EU's. That said, except in times of crisis, this region does not crack the top ten in terms of the areas of coordination and cooperation between the U.S. and EU. However, the potential for U.S.-EU coordination is considerable. Most recently, the two have engaged in the Armenia-Azerbaijan conflict in a coordinated fashion, President Michel and Secretary of State Antony Blinken alternating in convening the leaders of the two countries with a view to achieve a resolution to the conflict. The specific capabilities and strengths of the U.S. and EU could combine well to advance a more coherent Western presence in the region.

Historically, the EU sought to coordinate its activity in the Caucasus and Central Asia also with Russia. At the very least, the EU sought to maintain an open channel of communication with Russia about its presence in the region, in order to avoid unnecessary conflict. But Russia's zero-sum logic soon made that approach impracticable. In 2009, when the Eastern Partnership was launched, Russian Foreign Minister Sergey Lavrov termed the initiative an effort by the EU to establish a "Sphere of Influence."[2] He repeated this allegation in 2014 with regard to Ukraine.[3] From 2014 onward, it became clear that there was little space for coordination with Russia. As recently as June 2023, Lavrov stated in Tajikistan that Europe had "chosen a war path" with Russia, and lambasted Western development assistance to Central Asia as "tools for controlling and reformatting the political and economic landscape of the region for itself."[4]

With China, the EU's relationship is more complicated. The EU and China are each other's largest trading partners, at almost $2 billion in trade per day, but the relationship has become increasingly complicated over recent years. Part of the rationale for the EU's policy toward Central Asia has been related to connectivity and to EU-China trade, but over time has shifted in a way that has seen the EU increasingly seeking to not only complement Chinese connectivity projects in Central Asia, but provide a more sustainable alternative to them. The EU, meanwhile, has not been able to match the sheer scale of funding that China has been willing to provide.

The EU is very open about the problems in its relations with China, in April 2022 releasing a fact sheet that states that relations

---

2   "EU expanding its 'sphere of influence,' Russia says," EU observer, March 21, 2009. (https://euob-server.com/world/27827)

3   "Russia accuses EU of seeking Ukraine 'sphere of influence,'" Reuters, February 14, 2014. (https://www.reuters.com/article/us-ukraine-russia-eu-idUSBREA1D0PT20140214)

4   "Lavrov accuses Europe of choosing 'path of war' with Russia," Anadolu Agency, June 6, 2023. (https://www.aa.com.tr/en/asia-pacific/lavrov-accuses-europe-of-choosing-path-of-war-with-rus-sia/2915744)

have deteriorated, but that the EU "continues to deal with China simultaneously as a partner for cooperation and negotiation, an economic competitor and a systemic rival."[5]

There is potential for greater EU-Turkey coordination on Central Asia and the Caucasus, however. As with the U.S., the EU shares many interests with Turkey in this region. However, the poor state of EU-Turkish relations as a result of the infected Turkish bid for EU membership, along with the tensions between the two sides over refugee flows, has reduced the scope for such coordination. It remains to be seen whether the EU and Turkey can find ways to cooperate on policy toward this region following the re-election of President Erdogan, amid expectations that Turkish relations with the West will improve as a result of the economic needs in Turkey.

Future Trajectory

The EU's approach to the region has been increasing and broadening in a linear way since the mid-2000s. The EU, furthermore, has developed a systematic process to guide its policy toward these regions. This provides a considerable level of predictability to EU policy in the region. This approach compares favorably to the more disorganized policy of the United States. The EU's systematic approach has allowed it to avoid the pitfall of U.S. policy, namely to treat Central Asia and the Caucasus as a corollary to policies on other issues or powers rather than as a goal in itself. The EU has defined its relations with the region on the basis of its interests in the region itself, and not as an appendix to something else.

The EU faces challenges, of course. First among them is the fact that the EU is competing in a world of hard power, whereas

---

5   European External Action Service, "EU China Relations," Fact Sheet, April 2022. (https://www.eeas.europa.eu/sites/default/files/documents/EU-China_Factsheet_01Apr2022.pdf)

it does not inherently possess hard power. Traditionally, the EU has been focused more on soft power, economic cooperation, and the effort to use its normative power to support positive change in regions on its periphery. But as has been clear in recent years, the EU has understood the need to adapt to a world where hard power not only remains key but has been increasingly prominent. Turkey, for example, inserted itself into the South Caucasus through the provision of hard power in the Armenia-Azerbaijani conflict, and also has concluded defense and intelligence agreements with Central Asian states. The EU does not have the ability to compete in this regard. But that may also be its advantage. In Central Asia in particular, the EU's lack of hard power may make it easier for regional states to partner with the EU, as compared with the United States. The EU also has much to offer to countries that seek to embark on systemic reforms, particularly if it strengthens its resolve to also support reform in the security sector of these countries.

India's Changing Approach towards Central Asia and the Caucasus after the Afghanistan Debacle and the War in Ukraine

Gulshan Sachdeva

India's ambition to raise its profile and connect with Central Asian neighbourhood was reflected through its 'Extended Neighbourhood' and 'Connect Central Asia' policies. Prime Minister Modi further elevated these policies through India's SCO membership and other institutional mechanisms. India's strategy towards the region has been linked to its Afghanistan, China and Pakistan policies as well as Russian and U.S. designs. With the Afghanistan debacle, the earlier connectivity strategies are no longer valid as a Taliban-Pakistan-China axis will further strengthen the BRI profile, in which India has not participated. India's response to Ukraine war is almost identical to Central Asian States. Although India's relevance for Central Asia has increased for Central Asia after the war, New Delhi's options are limited. In coming years, India will work with Central Asian partners to safeguard the region from negative repercussions of the Taliban takeover in terms of radicalization, increased terrorist activity and drug trafficking.

Central Asia and the Caucasus have long been part of the Indian imagination because of old civilizational linkages and cultural connections. After the Soviet break-up, new geopolitical realities and geo-economic opportunities further influenced Indian thinking in the 1990s. The emergence of new independent states opened opportunities for energy imports as well as trade and transit. There were also worries of rising religious fundamentalism. Therefore, developing political, economic and energy partnerships dominated New Delhi's "extended neighbourhood" policy in the 1990s. Although India established close political ties with all countries in the region, economic ties remained limited. An unstable Afghanistan and difficult India-Pakistan relations created problems for direct connectivity. New Delhi tried to resolve the issue through working with Russia and Iran via the International North-South Trade Corridor (INSTC) and its tributaries. Due to the U.S.-Iran tensions and stagnating India-Russia trade, this option did not prove very effective. In the meanwhile, the Chinese profile in the region increased significantly.

Worried by its limited footprint in the region, India wholeheartedly supported the U.S. New Silk Road Strategy announced by Hillary Clinton in Chennai in 2011. Unlike the U.S., the EU and many multilateral organizations seeking to spread democracy and market economics, India primarily focused on ensuring political stability in the region. New Delhi obviously would have welcomed a more democratic Central Asia, but it favoured the process of democratization to happen at its own pace. For quite some time, New Delhi also remained convinced that Russia would retain a predominant political and economic influence in the region, and

---

1   Hillary Rodham Clinton, *Remarks on India and the United States: A Vision for the 21st Century*, Chennai, July 20, 2011. https://2009-2017.state.gov/secretary/20092013clinton/rm/2011/07/168840.htm

generally pursued cooperation with Moscow in Central Asia and the Caucasus. With increased U.S. interest in the region due to the Afghanistan conflict, some of India's security and economic interests also coincided with Washington's. In 2012, India announced its own twelve point 'Connect Central Asia' policy.[2] The idea was to strengthen India's political, security, economic and cultural connections throughout the region. Major initiatives included stepping up multilateral engagement (through the SCO and Eurasian Economic Union); establishing a new Central Asian University in Bishkek; setting up a Central Asian e-network with its hub in India; reactivating INSTC and close consultations on Afghanistan. The idea was to look at the region collectively in a more proactive manner. However, instead of looking at Central Asia and the Caucasus in its own right, Indian policy toward the region has been subservient to its Afghanistan, China and Pakistan policies. In addition, Russian and U.S. designs have further influenced Indian strategy towards the region.

Renewed Focus under Prime Minister Modi

Coinciding with economic transformation towards a market economy in the post-Soviet states, India also transitioned from an excessively inward-oriented to a more globally-integrated economy in the 1990s. As a result of new policies, it became one of the fastest growing economies in the world. High economic growth had its own strategic consequences. This helped India to strengthen its traditional partnerships with the developing world and also forge new partnerships with all major powers including the U.S., EU and Russia. New Delhi also signed many trade

---

2   Ministry of External Affairs, *India's 'Connect Central Asia' Policy: Keynote address by MOS Shri E. Ahamed at First India-Central Asia Dialogue*, June 12, 2012. https://www.mea.gov.in/Speech-es-Statements.htm?dtl/19791/

agreements in Asia. Apart from the "special and privileged" partnership with Russia within the Eurasian region, India signed four important strategic partnerships with Kazakhstan (2009), Uzbekistan (2011), Afghanistan (2011) and Tajikistan (2012).

Against this backdrop of an emerging India, Prime Minister Narendra Modi received a decisive mandate in the 2014 parliamentary elections. His Bharatiya Janata Party (BJP) campaigned on the promise to further boost economic growth and decisive foreign policy. This was also the time when many developments were taking place in the Eurasian region. As a result of rising tensions with the West over the initial Ukrainian crisis, Russia renewed its assertiveness in the post-Soviet space. For linking South and Central Asia through Afghanistan, the U.S. had announced its New Silk Road Strategy. However, it also declared its intention to exit from Afghanistan. China had already announced its Silk Road Economic Belt and 21st Century Maritime Silk Road, which turned into the Belt and Road Initiative (BRI). The landmark Iranian nuclear deal with the prospects of removal of sanctions against Tehran by the U.S. raised Indian hopes to further improve its profile in the region. Due to difficult India-Pakistan relations, Iran always plays a significant role in Indian strategic thinking towards Afghanistan, Central Asia and the Caucasus.

Worried about Russia and China and their increasing closeness, Central Asian regimes also started looking for enhanced strategic and economic engagement from India. This fits well within their 'multi-vector' foreign policies, in which they are trying to balance their relations with Russia and China through enhanced engagement with the West and regional players. The announcement of a U.S. withdrawal from Afghanistan from 2014 onward had already added a new dimension to India's relations with the region. It was becoming clearer that any failure of the Afghanistan project would pose common security challenges to both India and Central Asia. Relative stability in Afghanistan, on the other hand, would open up many economic opportunities to the region.

In July 2015, Prime Minister Narendra Modi visited all five Central Asian States. This was the first visit of any Indian prime minister to all the Central Asian countries together since they became independent in 1991. During the visit, 22 agreements were signed with five Central Asian countries. Apart from agreements on defence, military and technical cooperation, trade, tourism, culture etc, a bilateral agreement was also signed for the purchase of uranium from Kazakhstan. The visit resulted in a raised Indian profile in Central Asia. In December 2015, Indian Vice president Hamid Ansari attended the ground-breaking ceremony of the Turkmenistan-Afghanistan-Pakistan-India (TAPI) gas pipeline at Mary, Turkmenistan. There were hopes that pipeline may start operating by the end of 2018.

In June 2017, India also became a full member of the SCO. India has been an observer in the organisation since 2005. Prime Minister Modi had already signed a Memorandum of Obligation at the SCO Tashkent summit in 2016. During Prime Minister Modi's visit to Iran in May 2016, a trilateral agreement on Chabahar between India, Iran and Afghanistan was signed. Another contract for the development of Chabahar port was aimed to improve India's connectivity to Afghanistan and Central Asia. In 2018, India also joined the Ashgabat Agreement, which aimed to improve Eurasian connectivity and coordinate activities with other transport corridors including the INSTC. The agreement was first signed by Uzbekistan, Turkmenistan, Iran, Oman and Qatar in 2011. Kazakhstan and Pakistan also joined in 2016.

In 2019, New Delhi initiated an "India-Central Asia Dialogue" at the Foreign Ministers level including Afghanistan.[3] The first such dialogue took place in Samarkand which mainly focused on connectivity and ways to stabilize Afghanistan. During the same year, bilateral relations with Kyrgyzstan were also elevated to 'strategic partnership'. To improve development activities in the region, India also proposed setting up of an 'India-Central Asia Development Group' in addition to proposing dialogue on air corridors between India and Central Asia. February 2020 saw the creation of an India-Central Asia Business Council.[4] At the second India Central Asia Dialogue in October 2020, a $1 billion Line of Credit for development projects in infrastructure, IT, energy and agriculture was launched.[5] In 2020-21, bilateral trade between India and Central Asia was in the range of about $3 billion, out of which $2.5 billion was only with Kazakhstan. A large part of Kazakh imports to India were petroleum products, which have come down recently. India has another $700 million in bilateral trade with the Caucasus region.

Focus Area and Countries

In the last fifteen years, India's Afghanistan engagement had a direct bearing on its Central Asia policy. The South Caucasus has received much less attention and New Delhi does not have

---

3   Ministry of External Affairs, "Press Statement by EAM after First India-Central Asia Dialogue", January 13, 2019. https://www.mea.gov.in/Speeches-Statements.htm?dtl/30907/Press_Statement_by_EAM_After_1st_IndiaCentral_Asia_Dialogue

4   Outlook India, "India-Central Asia Business Council Launched" 6 February 2020. https://www.outlookindia.com/newsscroll/indiacentral-asia-business-council-launched/1727841

5   Ministry of External Affairs, "Joint Statement of the 2nd Meeting of the India-Central Asia Dialogue", October 28, 2020. (https://www.mea.gov.in/bilateral-documents.htm?dtl/33148/Joint+Statement+of+the+2nd+meeting+of+the+IndiaCentral+Asia+Dialogue)

any clearly articulated Caucasus policy. Although India is trying to formulate and implement a regional policy, bilateral ties have also been important for specific reasons. Tajikistan, for example, is very important strategically. It is about twenty kilometers from Greater Kashmir, separated by the narrow Wakhan corridor in Afghanistan. It is close to the Karakoram highway and camps of anti-India terrorist groups in Pakistan. India operated a medical facility at Farkhor base for the Northern Alliance which fought the Taliban in the 1990s. Along with Tajik forces, India also maintains an air base at Ayni, near Dushanbe, since 2002. During the current Taliban takeover, this base was used to evacuate Indian citizens from Afghanistan.⁶ Kazakhstan and Turkmenistan have been important for energy. TAPI has been part of the narrative for the last twenty years. Indian public sector company ONGC Videsh had invested about $300 million in Satpayev block in Kazakhstan. However, in 2018 the company exited Kazakhstan as it could not find commercially exploitable oil.⁷ Currently the ONGC holds stakes in Azeri Chirag Guneshi (ACG) fields and BTC pipeline in Azerbaijan. By contrast, Uzbekistan has been important for historical and political reasons. With increasing interests from Indian students, farmers and tourists in the Caucasus region, India's External Affairs Minister visited Georgia in 2021.⁸ Earlier he also visited Armenia.

In January 2022, Prime Minister Modi hosted a virtual

---

6 Snehesh Alex Philip, "Gissar Military Aerodrome — India's First Overseas Base that Came to the Rescue in Afghan Crisis" *The Print*, 23 August, 2021. https://theprint.in/defence/gissar-military-aero-drome-indias-first-overseas-base-that-came-to-the-rescue-in-afghan-crisis/720356/

7 The Economic Times, "ONGC Videsh to Exit Kazakhstan's Satpayev Oil Block" September 18, 2018. https://energy.economictimes.indiatimes.com/news/oil-and-gas/ongc-videsh-to-exit-kazakhstans-satpayev-oil-block/65856935

8 Ministry of External Affairs, "Statement by External Affairs Minister at the Joint Press Conference with H.E. Irakli Garibashvili, Prime Minister of Georgia", July 10, 2021. https://mea.gov.in/outo-ging-visit-detail.htm?34007/Statement+by+External+Affairs+Minister+at+the+Joint+Press+Confer-ence+with+HE+Irakli+Garibashvili+Prime+Minister+of+Georgia

summit with all five Central Asian presidents. At the summit it was decided to hold such summit every two years. Many proposals in the areas of trade, connectivity, security, development cooperation, defence and cultural and people to people contacts were agreed. To institutionalize and monitor the process, it was also agreed to set up an India-Central Asia Secretariat at New Delhi. Throughout the Central Asia and the Caucasus, India has a significant soft power influence through Bollywood, education exchanges and development cooperation projects.

The Afghanistan Debacle

With the Taliban taking over Afghanistan again, India will have to re-work its Central Asia strategy. The Afghanistan debacle is a major strategic setback for those countries which worked along with the U.S. in Afghanistan for the last 20 years. This includes not just NATO allies of the U.S., but also India. The immediate impact will be felt in the neighbouring regions of South and Central Asia. The current strategic environment surrounding Afghanistan is very different from the situation in the 1990s up until 2001. For India, the problem is complicated by the emergence of the Taliban-Pakistan-China axis as well as Russian, Turkish and Iranian support to the Taliban. Besides, direct 'engagement' by the EU and some of its member states risks providing *de facto* legitimacy to Pakistani designs in South and Central Asia.

It is only a matter of time before Taliban get recognition in one form or another from major powers. Pakistan, China, Russia, Turkey and Qatar, among other, are trying to facilitate their global engagements and interactions. The U.S. had already legitimized

---

9   Press Information Bureau, Government of India, "India-Central Asia Virtual Summit", 27 January 2022. https://pib.gov.in/PressReleasePage.aspx?PRID=1793068

the Taliban by signing an agreement with the movement in February 2020. The EU and its Member States have now agreed for an "operational engagement"[10] with the new government through a joint EU presence in Kabul coordinated by the European External Action Service. The UK also intends to have direct engagement with the Taliban.[11] Uzbekistan and Turkmenistan have been building links with the Taliban for some time, and a Kyrgyzstani delegation has also met the Taliban leadership[12]. Tajikistan, however, will keep pushing for an inclusive government with appropriate Tajik representation. The Taliban have started talking favorably about the TAPI and other connectivity projects with Central Asian neighbors.[13]

For the time being, Afghanistan is likely to be an extension of Pakistan. India will be planning accordingly. The whole world knows about the Taliban's linkages with Islamabad. It is not that Europe and the U.S. are naïve. But for most of them, strategically it does not matter now or they feel it does not pose an immediate direct threat to them. After two decades of American-led Western intervention, *The Economist* in its editorial claims that "Afghanistan is a backwater, with little geopolitical or economic significance."[14]

In the emerging scenario, India may find itself in a relatively disadvantageous position in Afghanistan and Central Asian

10 Alexandra Brzozowski, "EU Sets Five Conditions for Future 'Operational Engagement' with Taliban, September 3, 2021. https://www.euractiv.com/section/defence-and-security/news/eu-sets-five-conditions-for-future-operational-engagement-with-taliban/

11 Kim Sengupta, "Afghanistan: It's Time to Engage with the Taliban, Says Raab" *Independent*, 3 September 2021. https://www.independent.co.uk/asia/south-asia/raab-afghanistan-taliban-dialogue-b1913153.html

12 RFL/RL Kyrgyz Service, "Top Kyrgyz Officials Meet With Taliban Leadership In Kabul" September 23, 2021. https://gandhara.rferl.org/a/kyrgyz-taliban-meeting/31474821.html

13 Vladimir Afanasiev, "Taliban: Tapi Gas Pipeline Is a Priority Project" 18 August 2021. https://www.upstreamonline.com/production/taliban-tapi-gas-pipeline-is-a-priority-project/2-1-1053761

14 The Economist, "America Should Engage with the Taliban, Very Cautiously" September 4, 2021. https://www.economist.com/leaders/2021/09/02/america-should-engage-with-the-taliban-very-cautiously

region. This is the price India has to pay for going too close to the U.S. and certain errors in its own policy judgements. Even when every country, including the U.S., legitimised the Taliban politically by openly talking to them, Indian policy makers remained hesitant.

Despite the U.S. announcement of its withdrawal since 2014, New Delhi hoped the stalemate would continue for some more years. Now the new security and economic architecture in Afghanistan is going to be different from the one followed by Kabul in the last 20 years. The new influencers, particularly China, Pakistan, Russia and Iran, will be happy to see the U.S. influence reduced further. China and Pakistan will also try to minimise Indian engagement.

For India, Afghanistan's major strategic significance has been in the context of difficult India-Pakistan relations. Once Kabul is closely linked with the Pakistani state, its own strategic significance will decline. However, India's Pakistan problem will become bigger.

For India, Afghanistan has also been important for regional connectivity. The whole idea of the U.S. New Silk Road Strategy was to link Central Asia and South Asia (especially India) via Afghanistan through trade, transit and energy routes. Investments at the Chabahar port in Iran and the Zaranj-Delaram Road in Afghanistan were part of the strategy to bypass Pakistan. This approach is no longer valid, and as a result, India has to sort out its connectivity issues with China and Pakistan first before thinking about connectivity towards Central Asia via Afghanistan.

Afghanistan will continue to be important for regional connectivity. But now the focus may change towards China's BRI and the Gwadar port in Pakistan. Even under the Ghani government,

Kabul was keen on connecting itself to the BRI either directly or through the China-Pakistan Economic Corridor (CPEC). As Central Asians are already part of the BRI, they may find these developments useful. Taliban have already asserted that "China is our most important partner and represents a fundamental and extraordinary opportunity for us because it is ready to invest and rebuild our country."[15]

Just before the Taliban takeover, the Biden administration had agreed to set up a new quadrilateral diplomatic platform focused on enhancing regional connectivity involving the U.S., Afghanistan, Pakistan and Uzbekistan. In the changed circumstances, the Chinese may replace the U.S. as leaders in regional connectivity platforms involving Afghanistan. China-Russia bonhomie is matured now. Together their influence in Central Asian states is significant. Due to the U.S. obsession with Iran, Tehran will also work mainly with Russia and China. Iran will also become a formal SCO member soon.[16]

New Delhi is still mainly trying to coordinate its Afghanistan policy with the United States. But the U.S. and the broader West will have a very limited interest in Afghanistan in the coming years. Compared to Biden's "America is back" foreign policy promise[17], the exact opposite has happened in South Asia. To counter China's rise, India may aspire to work with the U.S. in the Indo-Pacific, but it will have a tough time finding convergences with the China-Pakistan-Taliban axis in South and Central Asia. In a shrinking space, it will still try to coordinate some of its

---

15   The Mint, "China is Our Most Important Partner, Says Taliban, September 3, 2021. https://www.livemint.com/news/india/china-is-our-most-important-partner-say-taliban-11630662700353.html

16   Maziar Motamedi "What Iran's Membership of Shanghai Cooperation Organisation Means" AlJazeera, 19 September 2021. https://www.aljazeera.com/news/2021/9/19/iran-shanghai-cooperation-organisation

17   The White House, "Remarks by President Biden in Address to a Joint Session of Congress" April 28, 2021. https://www.whitehouse.gov/briefing-room/speeches-remarks/2021/04/29/remarks-by-president-biden-in-address-to-a-joint-session-of-congress/

actions with Russia and Iran in Eurasia. In November 2021, the national security advisors of India, Russia, Iran and Central Asian republics met in Delhi to discuss evolving Afghanistan situation and threats arising from terrorism, radicalisation and drug trafficking in the region.[18] They again met in Dushanbe in May 2022 and Moscow in February 2023 respectively. So far, this Regional Security Dialogue on Afghanistan has had five meetings. The first two meetings were held in Iran. China has also participated in the last two meetings. Besides, countries also exchange views at Afghanistan Contact Group within the SCO.[19] During President Putin's visit to India in December 2021, it was asserted that both India and Russia share "common perspectives and concerns on Afghanistan."[20]

To get recognition and assistance, earlier it was expected that the Taliban may allow restricted female education and token women presence in offices. Despite some initial positive statements, their situation has regressed to pre-2002 levels.[21] Besides, their links with terror groups will continue be a serious concern. New Delhi will also have to live with Pakistan's perceived success in its adventure in Afghanistan and its implications for the Indian national security and Central Asia strategy. India's declared policy is 'wait and watch.'[22] It has been carefully monitoring Taliban's

18 Ministry of External Affairs, "Delhi Declaration on Afghanistan" November 10, 2021. https://mea.gov.in/bilateral-documents.htm?dtl/34491/Delhi_Declaration_on_Afghanistan

19 Ayjaz Wani, *Regional Multilateral Consultations on Afghanistan*, Raisina Debates, Observer Research Foundation, 17 February 2023. https://www.orfonline.org/expert-speak/regional-multilateral-consultations-on-afghanistan/

20 Ministry of External Affairs, "21st India – Russia Annual Summit", December 06, 2021. https://mea.gov.in/press-releases.htm?dtl/34608/21st_India__Russia_Annual_Summit

21 UN Office of the High Commissioner of Human Rights, "Afghanistan: UN Experts say 20 Years of Progress for Women and Girls' Rights Erased since Taliban Takeover", 8 March 2023, https://www.ohchr.org/en/press-releases/2023/03/afghanistan-un-experts-say-20-years-progress-women-and-girls-rights-erased

22 The Hindu, "India Adopting 'Wait and Watch' Policy on Afghanistan, Says Government" August 26, 2021, https://www.thehindu.com/news/national/jaishankar-briefs-political-leaders-on-afghanistan-situation/article36112751.ece

links with Pakistan based terror groups. The Taliban government, even under Pakistani influence, will need broader recognition and economic opportunities arising from Indian linkages. Although neither the Indian government nor the Taliban are in a hurry to change their perceptions about each other, a limited engagement has already happened. Reports indicate that a 'technical team' has been placed in the Indian embassy in Kabul and some humanitarian assistance has been provided [23].

The War in Ukraine

Although not directly relevant, the war in Ukraine may create a new dynamic in India-Central Asia relations. Indian and Central Asian positions on the Ukraine war are almost identical to each other. New Delhi and Central Asians have neither condemned nor endorsed Russian actions in Ukraine; they have not joined western sanctions against Russia; and none of them is going to recognise any of the annexed parts as part of Russia. Though sympathetic to Russia, India and Central Asian also have good relations with Ukraine and support its unity and territorial integrity. Although on the sidelines of the SCO summit in Samarkand in September 2022, Prime Minister Modi told President Putin that "today's era is not of war," [24] India's fundamental position on Ukraine war has not changed much.

Since the Ukraine war, trade between Russia and Central Asia has increased significantly. [25] Similarly, India-Russia trade

---

23 The Print, "Taliban Open to Indian Investment Including in Urban Infrastructure, Says Report" 23 December 2022. https://theprint.in/world/taliban-open-to-indian-investment-including-in-urban-infrastructure-report/1278185/

24 Suhasini Haidar, "PM Modi Tells Vladimir Putin 'Now is Not an Era of War'" The Hindu, 17 September 2022, https://www.thehindu.com/news/national/pm-modi-holds-talks-with-russian-president-vladimir-putin-on-sidelines-of-samarkand-sco-summit/article65899314.ece

25 Johan Engvall, "Central Asia One Year After Russia's Full-Scale Invasion of Ukraine", The Central Asia Caucasus Analyst, 7 March 2023, https://www.cacianalyst.org/resources/pdf/23307_FT_Engvall_2.pdf

which was hovering around $10 billion a year for many years, is likely to touch $50 billion in 2023-24. This is largely on the basis of discounted oil purchases from Russia. In fact, Russia has already become India's top oil supplier. In March 2023, India's crude oil imports from Russia were 1.64 million barrels per day.[26] Although this is a dynamic situation, it may have long term strategic consequences for Eurasia. Despite political commitment from India, Iran and Russia, the International North South Trade Corridor (INSTC) was not able to take off due to low India-Russia trade volumes. If India-Russia trade continues to be in this range, traders may finally start using the INSTC. Many of them were reluctant earlier due to low trade volumes. India would also like to link this corridor to Chabahar port in Iran where India has been involved for many years. Through various INSTC tributaries, India's connections with Central Asia and the Caucasus could also be strengthened. As Ukraine war and US-China tensions have pushed Russia and China further closer, Central Asians are uncomfortable. They would like to strengthen their economic links with India. Indian policy makers are aware of these opportunities but are constrained by limited regional geopolitics and US sanctions against Russian and Iran.

Changing Approach

In the last three decades, India had an ambition to raise its profile and connect with its Central Asian neighbourhood. This was reflected through its 'Extended Neighbourhood' and 'Connect Central Asia' policy. Though New Delhi was successful in forging close strategic ties with the region, the instability in Afghanistan

---

26   The Mint, "India's Russian Oil Imports now Double of Nation's Top Oil Supplier Iraq" 9 April 2023, https://www.livemint.com/news/india/indias-russian-oil-imports-now-double-of-nation-s-top-oil-supplier-iraq-11681022557146.html

and the troubles in India-Pakistan relations did not allow New Delhi to seriously connect economically to Central Asia and the Caucasus. The increasing Chinese profile in the region also coincided with a significant U.S. engagement in Central Asia due to Afghanistan. To improve its connectivity, New Delhi continued making efforts along with Russia, Iran and Afghanistan. The INSTC, Chabahar port and engagements in Afghan infrastructure was part of this strategy. The U.S. design to connect Central and South Asia through Afghanistan coincided with Indian policy. Though it did not take off, it helped foster a positive connectivity narrative. With the U.S. debacle in Afghanistan, these narratives are no longer valid. The Taliban-Pakistan-China axis will now strengthen the BRI profile. This is happening at a time when India's relations with both China and Pakistan are at an all-time low. Indian and central Asian positions to the war in Ukraine are almost identical. Although the situation has opened some new opportunities, India's options in the region are limited. India's growing ties with the U.S. in the Indo-Pacific may also restrict its options in Central Asia and the Caucasus. In the next few years, India will work with Central Asians to safeguard the region from negative repercussions of Taliban takeover in terms of radicalization, increased terrorist activity and drug trafficking. This was clearly evident when at the SCO summit in 2021 where Prime Minister Modi asserted that biggest challenges in the region "are related to peace, security and trust-deficit and the root cause of these problems is increasing radicalization."[27] The war in Ukraine and India's SCO presidency in 2023 may offer some opportunities for India to improve its security and connectivity linkages with the region.

---

27 Ministry of External Affairs, "Prime Minister's Address at the Plenary Session of the 21st Meeting of SCO Council of Heads of State" September 17, 2021. https://mea.gov.in/Speeches-Statements. htm?dtl/34274/Prime_Ministers_Address_at_the_Plenary_Session_of_the_21st_Meeting_of_SCO_Council_of_Heads_of_State

Japan as no "other": Decolonizing Alternative for Central Asia?

Timur Dadabaev

Japan has been one of the first and most consistent partners of Central Asian (Central Asia) states in supporting their nation-building and regionalism. It was also the first country to propose the concept of the Silk Road to build interconnectedness and open partnerships for regional states. In this sense, the Japanese presence in the Central Asia region represents an engagement for diversifying and decolonizing Central Asia states' relations with international partners. While Japan has been active through its ODA policy in the region, recent years demonstrate how Japan attempts to reconceptualize its engagement in Central Asia by promoting international partnerships with the EU to utilize mutual strengths to dynamize the EU and the Japanese presence in Central Asia. Through regional and bilateral connections, Japan is attempting to empower these regional states while also changing its own approaches to international cooperation.

Over the past 30 years, the Japanese approach to Central Asia has been to secure the Japanese presence in the region by offering Central Asian nations an additional option of an international partner among traditional choices, such as Russia, and, in most recent history, China. The schemes offered to facilitate engagement between Japan and Central Asia were vibrant and diverse, reflecting the changing realities of the Central Asian region and the changing role and perception of the "self" in Japan.[1] As is well documented in previous studies, the search for engagement schemes started with the 1996 Obuchi mission to Azerbaijan and Central Asia, spearheaded by the Member of Parliament and later Prime Minister Keizo Obuchi, which produced a strong endorsement of wider engagement of Japan in the region. It resulted in P.M. Ryutaro Hashimoto's 1997 Eurasian/Silk Road Diplomacy speech, in which the concept of the Silk Road was first used as a geopolitical concept, embracing Central Asian states, China, Russia and Japan in an imagined net of interdependence.[2] While the administrations of P.M. Obuchi (1998-1999) and P.M. Yoshirō Mori (1999-2000) did not proactively engage with the Central Asia region, it was P.M. Junichiro Koizumi's administration (2001-2006) that aimed to aggressively shake up the Japanese approach to this region by announcing the Central Asia + Japan Dialogue Forum, a set of annual inter-ministerial and high-level talks to support Central Asian regional integration and to facilitate a larger corporate presence for Japanese corporate interests, in the face of growing Chinese and Russian pressures. The particular

---

1   See Timur Dadabaev, *Japan in Central Asia: Strategies, Initiatives, and Neighboring Powers*, New York: Palgrave Macmillan, 2016; Sabina Insebayeva, "Japan's Central Asia Policy Revisited: National Identity, Interests, and Foreign Policy Discourses," *Nationalities Papers*, vol. 47 no. 5, 2019, pp. 853–867.

2   See Nikolay Murashkin, *Japan and the New Silk Road Diplomacy, Development and Connectivity*, New York: Routledge, 2020; Timur Dadabaev, *Transcontinental Silk Road Strategies: Comparing China, Japan and South Korea in Uzbekistan*, New York: Routledge, 2019.

importance of the Central Asia + Japan forum is that it offered an alternative option of a distant yet powerful external economic partner to the region, which did not display a neo-colonizing tendency or strive for domination, as was widely feared regarding China and Russia[3].

Most recently, PM Shinzo Abe (2013-2020) attempted to further dynamize Central Asia-Japan relations when he visited all Central Asian states and lobbied for larger participation of Japanese corporations in Central Asia. In his approach to strengthening Japanese competitiveness, PM Abe introduced the notion of high-quality infrastructure by arguing that Japanese infrastructure projects based on high-quality and sustainability standards[4] offer more sustainable and reliable alternatives (as compared to Chinese projects, for example) for developing countries inclusive of Central Asia states.

Visions of the Region and Japanese Foreign Policy

In approaching Central Asia, the Japanese government utilizes both multilateral and bilateral channels, which include extending its support to individual state-building efforts and encouraging regional cooperation through Central Asia + Japan, as described above. In doing so, the Japanese government aims to display a certain degree of sensitivity toward disparities between regional states while facilitating long-term regional consolidation in light of growing pressures by other large players, such as China and Russia. In this sense, Japanese support for Central Asian states can

---

3   For this point see Timur Dadabaev, *Decolonizing Central Asian International Relations: Beyond Empires*, New York: Routledge, 2021.

4   Shinzo Abe, "The Future of Asia: Be Innovative," Speech by Prime Minister Shinzo Abe at the Banquet of the 21st International Conference on the Future of Asia, May 21, 2015 (https://japan.kantei.go.jp/97_abe/statement/201505/0521foaspeech.html).

be likened to Japanese support for nation- and regional-building in the ASEAN region.

As Japan is also the largest provider of Official Development Assistance (ODA) in the region, its ODA focuses on the following areas:

- Modernization of the Soviet-era infrastructure.

- Promotion of industrial development and employment opportunities both in the region and in Japan.

- Support of governance reforms and institutions of the market economy as well as human resource development.

Regional states with significant mineral resources and human resource potential (such as Kazakhstan, Uzbekistan and Turkmenistan) remain the most important in terms of corporate interest for the Japanese business community. Kazakhstan retains the leading position in this aspect, with 52 Japanese companies registered in Kazakhstan (with interests in the areas of energy, finance, transportation, construction of infrastructures and trade sectors).[5] Some of these companies frequently use their successful engagements in Kazakhstan as a launching pad for expansion into neighboring Central Asian states, as exemplified by Uzbekistan.

While Kazakhstan is no longer a recipient of ODA assistance from Japan due to the increase in its economic indicators, the past (1993 to 2007) ODA assistance focused on the areas of support for policy formulation, institutional improvement,

---

5   For excellent analysis of the Japanese corporate advances in Central Asia and the challenges, see Manabu Shimoyashiro, "The current situation, challenge and perspective of the economic relations between Japan and Central Asia," *Roshia Toou Kenkyu (Russian and East European Studies)*, no. 49, 2020, pp. 82-91.

human resource development, economic and social infrastructure improvement, environment and disaster preparedness.

In regard to Turkmenistan, only 6 Japanese companies are registered in Turkmenistan, primarily focusing on its energy resource base symbolized by its enormous reserves of natural gas. Negotiations on wider Japanese participation in the construction of natural gas processing plants and other facilities were also held during PM Abe's visit in 2015, unfortunately with few practical outcomes.

However, post-Karimov Uzbekistan (after 2016) remains one of the countries generating the most enthusiastic expectations in Japan due to the change in its political environment, the Uzbek government's proactive position in attracting foreign partners and very strong pro-Japanese public sentiments, as demonstrated by a number of opinion polls.

In addition to being supported by 24 Japanese companies registered in Uzbekistan, bilateral relations with Uzbekistan are promoted by the large number of Japanese ODA projects (such as modernization of power plants) and the presence of the office of the Japan External Trade Organization (JETRO) in Tashkent, which is primarily responsible for data gathering and dissemination for Japanese companies interested in the Uzbek market. In line with ODA priorities, which often define corporate interests, Uzbekistan attracts Japanese public and private investments in the areas of the modernization of economic infrastructure (transportation, energy), human resource development and institution building for promoting the market economy and economic and industrial development. In addition, support for restructuring of the social sector (in areas such as agriculture, regional development, and health care) also prominently feature in the bilateral cooperation agenda.

Priorities and Potential Areas

Japan's contribution to making Central Asia states more self-reliant and regionally consolidated centers around five main areas: capacity development (to facilitate the trade and economic potential of these states), digital education and training development, energy resource processing and trade, modernization of energy facilities, and people-to-people cooperation.

Among the leading Japanese capacity development institutions in Central Asia are the Japan centers initially established in Uzbekistan, Kazakhstan and Kyrgyzstan under the Ministry of Foreign Affairs, which were later either transferred to local management (Almaty and Astana in Kazakhstan) or to the management of the JICA (in the case of Tashkent in Uzbekistan and Bishkek in Kyrgyzstan). They serve as institutions providing business courses (sometimes called mini-MBAs) taught by representatives of both the local and Japanese business communities, language courses and cultural exchange initiatives.

Qualitatively different are the training and education provided by the Japanese educational institutions and initiatives that aim to promote digital training education, exemplified by the Japan Digital University at the University of World Languages in Uzbekistan. Although it appears to be an educational institution, the Japanese partner that established it is the Japanese Digital Knowledge company, which focuses on the provision of digital products for educational purposes. The purpose of this type of Japanese training institution in Central Asia is to provide training to Central Asia youth, who can then find employment as programmers either distantly or by traveling to Japan after they graduate from the university. As a training scheme, it aims to both provide needed expertise to Central Asia youth and benefit the Japanese labor market, which is currently experiencing shortages in certain professions due to the rapidly growing population.[6]

Other educational and training initiatives are championed by private Japanese foundations, such as the Nippon Foundation, which funds the Nippon Foundation Central Asia-Japan Human Resource Development Project financing graduate studies for Central Asia youth in Japan. It also funds the Japan Central Asia Friendship Association (JACAFA) serving as the bridge between the graduates of Japan-trained programs.

In the energy sector, Japanese corporations have been active in establishing their presence in resource-rich countries, such as Kazakhstan and Turkmenistan, for the past 30 years. However, the new frontier for the Japanese corporate community comes with the Japanese government's drive toward decarbonization of the Japanese economy. While this drive diminishes the importance of the carbon energy-rich Central Asia region, it offers new opportunities for Japanese corporate communities to promote renewable energy technology in the Central Asia region. In particular, the projected fall in demand for natural gas and oil which would come with decarbonization pushes Central Asia states to develop their own responses, such as seeking to process their carbon-based energy resources into hydrogen. As outlined by the Presidential Decree (March 2021) and announced by the Ministry of Energy of Uzbekistan in 2021, the road map for developing hydrogen is now in process of being compiled in Uzbekistan. In

---

6   For patterns of educational migration from Uzbekistan to Japan see Timur Dadabaev, Shigeto Sonoda and Jasur Soipov, "A guest for a day? An analysis of Uzbek 'language migration' into the Japanese educational and labour markets," *Central Asian Survey*, vol. 40 no. 3, 2021, pp. 438-466.

addition, the same Presidential document established a National Research Institute on Renewables and Hydrogen and a laboratory for renewable and hydrogen energy technologies indicating the priorities that government sees for cooperation with foreign partners. As such, it is the first of its kind in Central Asia, and the Japanese support and assistance can be very timely.

Finally, infrastructure development has long been an area of interest to Japanese corporations, especially in light of the intensification of corporate competition for various projects between the Chinese, Russian, Korean and other business communities.[7]

In addition to corporate participation in such infrastructure development, Japan has the advantage of its important voice in international institutions, such as the Asian Development Bank and its CAREC (Central Asia Regional Economic Cooperation), which is a partnership of 11 countries (including five Central Asian countries, Azerbaijan and Georgia) facilitating multimodal transportation networks, free movement of people and freight, and various economic corridors.

The Uzbekistan-Afghanistan transit route can serve as one such project if the situation in Afghanistan stabilizes[8], as discussed during the Tashkent conference on connectivity between Central and South Asia, to which Japanese policymakers paid careful attention. However, the changing situation in Afghanistan prevents any long-term planning among the Japanese policy officials at this stage.[9]

---

7   Timur Dadabaev, *Chinese, Japanese and Korean In-roads into Central Asia: Comparative Analysis of the Economic Cooperation Road Maps for Uzbekistan*, Policy Studies Series. Honolulu, HI: East West Center, 2019.

8   For Japan's Afghan policy, see Jagannath Panda, "Tokyo and Taliban 2.0: Gauging Japan's Political Stake in Kabul," *Focus Asia: Perspective & Analysis*, 2021.

9   For important points to be considered by the Japanese government see Tomohiko Uyama, "Recommendations for responding to the situation in Afghanistan," Japan Forum on International Relations, 2021 (https://www.jflr.or.jp/j/activities/studygroup/2020/geopolitics/210907ut.htm).

Competitive Advantages of Japan in Central Asia

Japan faces a few challenges in Central Asia as it attempts to define the role and importance of Central Asia for its economy and society. While in the early 1990s, Central Asia was framed by the foreign policy of Japan as a region that could potentially provide much-needed energy resources for the Japanese market, the difficulties of logistics in delivering these resources to Japan, a range of Japan-unfriendly countries between Japan and Central Asia (China and Russia, for example) and the declining importance of carbon-based energy resources in Japan call for a new framing of the importance of the region. As importantly suggested by JETRO officials, there is a need to consider the prospects of shifting from the pattern of Japanese corporations reimporting products produced outside of Japan back into the Japanese market toward producing products made by Japanese corporations in third country markets for international consumers. The suggested concept is referred to as "Made by Japan in Central Asia" and is proposed by certain officials as a way to reframe the purposes of Japanese engagement in the Central Asia region and make use of the convenient geographic location and young and well-educated work force of the region to enhance the competitiveness of Japanese corporations internationally[10].

In addition to the need to reconceptualize Japanese involvement in the region, the hesitance of Japanese corporations to enter the Central Asian markets is another challenge. One aspect relates to the fact that large Japanese corporations with long traditions and knowledge of the Soviet, Russian and Central Asia markets consider the scale of the region and the margins to be gained

---

10 See Shimoyashiro, "The current situation, challenge and perspective of the economic relations between Japan and Central Asia," p. 90.

in it to be slimmer than those in Southeast Asia or Europe and therefore choose not to launch their businesses in Central Asia. Middle-sized and small enterprises that could have benefitted from Central Asia engagements do not have basic information, cultural fluency or experience in these markets, preventing them from challenging Central Asia frontiers. In this sense, the task of making the information[11] of both the JETRO and Central Asia governments available to Japanese corporations remains one of the key ones to facilitating the expansion of the corporate presence of Japanese companies in the region and offering more alternatives, which are currently often limited to Chinese, Korean, UAE, Russian and a few European corporations.

Japan as Central Asia's Third Partner

There are two potential trajectories of the Japanese presence in Central Asia in the nearest future. One trajectory depends on the ability of Japanese corporations and the government to define their competitive advantages in the Central Asia region compared to those of other powers. This also relates to how Japan can define not only what it can do for the Central Asian region but also what benefits it can gain from it. While Japanese corporations previously aimed to search for resources and products in Central Asia to import back to Japan, there is a need for a shift of this mentality to create a pattern of mutually beneficial relations when products produced by Japanese corporations in the region do not have to be imported back to the Japanese market but can rather target international markets. This can be accomplished in line with the concept of "Made by Japan in Central Asia" for international markets, as explained above.

---

11 Shimoyashiro, "The current situation, challenge and perspective of the economic relations between Japan and Central Asia," p. 89.

Another angle relates to the international partnerships of Japan with like-minded partners to increase Japan's competitiveness in the region when compared to China and Russia.[12] As a sign of such an approach, Japan is seeking alliances with other countries, as exemplified by its Strategic Partnership Agreement (SPA) with the European Union,[13] applied in February 2019.[14] The SPA provides the platform for cooperation between the EU and Japan in third regions, such as Central Asia, based on shared values of democracy, rule of law, human rights and fundamental freedoms[15]. The SPA framework supports cooperation between the EU and Japan in a wide range of areas, from promoting the market economy to financial policy, renewable energy, science and technology, among many others.[16] To complement the SPA, Japan and the EU signed an agreement on a Partnership on Sustainable Connectivity and Quality Infrastructure at the Europa Connectivity Forum held on 27 September 2019 in Brussels.[17] This allows Japan to further promote its standards of quality infrastructure and turn its apparent weakness of having costly technology into an advantage of offering high-quality know-how, in addition to paying careful attention to the needs of Central Asia nations in terms of debt alleviation and sustainability and financial, social

---

12 For EU comparison to China in Central Asia, see Fabienne Bossuyt, "Engaging with Central Asia: China Compared to the EU," in Jan Wouters, Jean-Christophe Defraigne and Matthieu Burnay, eds., *China, the European Union and the Developing World: A Triangular Relationship*, Cheltenham: Edward Elgar, 2015, pp. 210–235.

13 See Axel Berkofsky, *Moving Beyond Rhetoric? The EU–Japan Strategic Partnership Agreement (SPA)*, Stockholm: The Institute for Security and Development Policy, 2020 (https://isdp.eu/content/uploads/2020/04/EU-Japan-SPA-IB-09.04.20.pdf).

14 Ministry of Foreign Affairs of Japan, Japan–EU Strategic Partnership Agreement (SPA), Tokyo, 2018 (www.mofa.go.jp/files/000381944.pdf). Also see Ministry of Foreign Affairs of Japan, EU—Japan Strategic Partnership Agreement, February, 1, 2019 (https://eeas.europa.eu/sites/eeas/files/fact-sheet_eu-japan_strategic_partnership_agreement_japan.pdf).

15 For analysis of the Japan-EU cooperation in Central Asia see Timur Dadabaev, "Emerging Japan-EU strategic partnership and its implications for Central Asia," in *Decolonizing Central Asian International Relations*, 2021, pp.64-75.

16 Marie Söderberg, *EU–Japan Connectivity Promises*. European University Institute, 2021 (https://hdl.handle.net/1814/71619).

17 Ministry of Foreign Affairs of Japan. Partnership on Sustainable Connectivity and Quality Infrastructure Between Japan and the European Union, 2019 (https://www.mofa.go.jp/files/000521432.pdf).

and environmental sustainability. The European Investment Bank (EIB)[18], European Bank of Reconstruction and Development (EBRD), Asian Development Bank (ADB), Japan Bank of International Cooperation (JBIC)[19], and Nippon Export and Investment Insurance (NEXI)[20] and Japan International Cooperation Agency (JICA)[21] are considered the key actors in such cooperation, supporting the needs of the EU and Japanese corporate communities and governments.

18 European Investment Bank. EIB Expands its Partnership with Japan's JICA. 2019 (www.eib.org/en/press/news/eib-expands-partnership-with-japan).

19 Japan Bank for International Cooperation, "JBIC Signs MOU with European Investment Bank: Promoting cooperation between Japan and the EU to create business opportunities both in Europe and beyond," October 23, 2018, (https://www.jbic.go.jp/en/information/press/press-2018/1023-011505.html).

20 Nippon Export and Investment Insurance (NEXI), "MOU on Corporation between the EIB and NEXI," October 23, 2018 (www.nexi.go.jp/en/topics/newsrelease/2018102205.html).

21 Japan International Cooperation Agency (JICA), "Signing of Memorandum of Understanding with the European Investment Bank," October 18, 2019 (https://www.jica.go.jp/english/news/press/2019/20191018_41.html).

Bureaucratic Morass and Conceptual Pitfalls: America's Approach to Central Asia and the Caucasus

Svante E. Cornell

The Biden Administration's National Security Strategy illustrates the bureaucratic challenges to a more focused and efficient U.S. policy toward lands that do not fit snugly within the decades-old geographic concepts into which U.S. policymakers divide the world. This is particularly true for the geopolitically crucial areas from Turkey in the West to the Chinese border. Although U.S. strategy places great emphasis on strategic competition with Russia and China, it essentially ignores the areas between these powers, seemingly oblivious to the risk that America could once again be locked out of the Eurasian continent, and see hostile powers dominate the corridor to Europe and the Middle East. To remedy this, the U.S. must shake up its mental map of the world, and make bureaucratic adjustments accordingly.

In spite of the partisan gridlock in Washington, there is considerable continuity between the National Security Strategy released by the Trump Administration in 2018 and the most recent one published by the Biden Administration in October. The main defined threat to U.S. national security remains the same: the challenge posed by revisionist, authoritarian powers Russia and China to the United States and its interests. Another similarity between the two documents is the extent to which both pay scant attention to the region between these large powers.

This omission may seem natural, given that Central Asia and the Caucasus is a largely landlocked region of less than 100 million people in what some consider a remote part of the world. To that, few of the region's states are paragons of democracy. Still, if the United States truly aspires to answer the challenge posed by Russian and Chinese intentions, it cannot ignore the very area of the world where Russia and China meet, along with Turkey and Iran. This is the case not because of some nineteenth-century style zero-sum logic, but for very real strategic reasons. If it were locked out of Central Asia and the Caucasus, America's ability to respond to crises on the Eurasian continent would be strongly diminished. Indeed, without access to Georgian and Azerbaijani airspace and Central Asian bases, the U.S. would have been unable to mount such a rapid response to the Afghanistan-based terrorist forces responsible for targeting the American homeland. Looking ahead, Chinese and/or Russian domination of Central Asia would enable powers hostile to the United States to establish control of the areas connecting southward and westward to South Asia and the Middle East. This, in turn, would strongly shift the balance of power on the entire Eurasian continent. It would empower their partner, Iran. And it would lead hesitant American partners like Turkey and India to reconsider their loyalties.

For over a decade now, there is a strong perception across

Central Asia and the Caucasus that the U.S. has been disengaging from the region. The chaotic withdrawal from Afghanistan seemed to confirm this; unfortunately, it has not been followed by a meaningful American initiative to reassure regional states. True, the United States has a dialogue format called C5+1 with Central Asia's five states. And yes, after a long period of inattention, the U.S. is again involved in brokering a lasting solution to the Armenia-Azerbaijan conflict in the South Caucasus, which provides Central Asia with a connection to Turkey and Europe. But this pales in comparison to the rising levels and frequency with which other regional and world powers engage with the region. Vladimir Putin is a frequent visitor to the region, interacting with leaders there on a continuous basis. Chinese President Xi Jinping not only launched his signature Belt and Road Initiative in Central Asia back in 2013; this year, he made the region the destination of his first foreign trip following the Covid-19 pandemic. Turkey has boosted its engagement with the region as well: President Recep Tayyip Erdogan led a summit of the newly upgraded Organization of Turkic States as recently as November 2022. Heads of State of Japan, South Korea and India went on multi-country trips to the region before the pandemic and have resumed their interaction with Central Asia. As detailed elsewhere in this volume, the European Union has upgraded its ties to the region as well: European Commission President Ursula von der Leyen visited Azerbaijan in July 2022, and in 2022 and 2023 the President of the European Council, Charles Michel, joined summits with Central Asian Presidents in Astana and Cholpon-Ata.

Conspicuously missing from this picture is the United States. Secretary of State Antony Blinken hosted a meeting with his regional counterparts in New York in the fall of 2022 and flew to

Astana for the C5+1 meeting in February 2023. No U.S. President has yet visited Central Asia, and the last cabinet-level official to spend time in the region before Blinken's trip was Mike Pompeo in early 2020. In sum, every other regional or world power seems to view Central Asia as an important world region and makes it a priority to interact with the region at high levels. Only the United States stands out.

Why is this the case? There are likely many reasons, ranging from the dysfunction of American politics to the range of world issues a decimated foreign service must attend to. But a closer look at consecutive National Security Strategies, and at American policy more broadly, suggests there are simple, and fixable, bureaucratic reasons for America's lack of focus on the region.

Shifting National Security Strategies

A comparison of recent NSS documents is illustrative. In the 2006 NSS, Central Asia is termed "an enduring priority for our foreign policy," and the document pays specific attention to the task of connecting Central and South Asia through Afghanistan.[1] Interestingly, this disconnected the Caucasus from Central Asia in U.S. policy, something that in practice doomed U.S. efforts to bring about greater connectivity across the Caspian Sea.

The Obama Administration's first NSS, published in 2010, did not mention Central Asia at all – surely a surprise to readers in the region that had taken the mention of an "enduring priority" to heart. The next document, issued in February 2015, included the region only obliquely, when speaking of "advancing economic integration in South and Central Asia" in a passage focused on India

---

1   "National Security Strategy of the United States of America, 2006," p. 40. (https://www.comw.org/qdr/fulltext/nss2006.pdf)

and Pakistan.[2] By contrast, Central Asia reappeared in the 2017 NSS, published by Trump Administration. Here, the focus was on counter-terrorism cooperation and on helping build a region that is "resilient against domination by rival powers, resistant to becoming jihadist safe havens, and prioritize[s] reforms."[3] As for the adjoining Caucasus region, to the extent that it is mentioned at all throughout these documents, it is in the form a passing mention of America's contribution to conflict resolution in the region, or in the past, singling out Georgia's democratic achievements as worthy of support.

In the most recent NSS, there is half a paragraph of text on Central Asia, a fact that is undoubtedly positive. It is also reassuring that the U.S. commits to "continue to support the independence, sovereignty and territorial integrity of Central Asia." The document then lists areas of cooperation, which include adaptation to climate change, energy and food security, and continuing to cooperate within the C5+1 framework on regional cooperation. But while the document indicates an appreciation for the importance of security-related questions such as territorial integrity, there is no mention of security in the steps the U.S. is planning to engage in. The hard security realities faced by Central Asian states is a glaring omission in the various priority areas outlined in the document.

Bureaucratic Confusion

A cursory look at these strategies reveals a most troubling problem, which is replicated in American government bodies.

---

2 "National Security Strategy," February 2015, p. 25. (https://obamawhitehouse.archives.gov/sites/default/files/docs/2015_national_security_strategy_2.pdf).

3 "National Security Strategy of the United States of America," December 2017," p. 50. (https://trump-whitehouse.archives.gov/wp-content/uploads/2017/12/NSS-Final-12-18-2017-0905.pdf)

Whereas the U.S. Government classifies the South Caucasus as part of Europe, it has yet to decide where Central Asia belongs. The 2006 NSS – which provided the clearest statement of U.S. interests in Central Asia – put the region under the of "South and Central Asia," a novel geographic concept that followed the U.S. war in Afghanistan. This occurred in parallel with the creation in the State Department of a new Bureau of South and Central Asian affairs (SCA), thus removing Central Asia from the Europe bureau. This move made sense from an American perspective: it followed the inclusion of Central Asia in the U.S. military's Central Command (CENTCOM), and it enabled the U.S. to have the areas to Afghanistan's north and south in the same geographic unit. As the 2006 NSS states, it also enables the U.S. to work for the opening of trade routes connecting Central Asia to the south, which for millennia had been the landlocked region's main window to the world. A similar restructuring took place in the National Security Council.

As mentioned, the 2010 NSS did not mention Central Asia at all – a major shift, giving the 2006 document's identification of the region as an "enduring priority." When it reappeared in the 2015 NSS, it was as a cursory mention under a broad Asia-Pacific heading. The 2018 NSS once again, as in the Bush Administration, had the region under a "South and Central Asia" heading; but to find Central Asia in the most recent document, the reader must look at the very end of the "Europe" heading, introduced with the curious phrase "elsewhere in Eurasia."

The U.S. bureaucracy has seen similar fluctuations. In the State Department, the SCA Bureau has remained in place since its creation almost twenty years ago, and provide a modicum of continuity. Not so in the National Security Council. The Obama

Administration made Central Asia the purview of the Senior Director for Russian affairs at the NSC. The Trump Administration moved Central Asia back with South Asia, as in the State Department; and after some initial hesitation, the Biden Administration reverted to the Obama Administration's view of the world, placing the region under Russia. Meanwhile, the South Caucasus has remained throughout this period a largely forgotten part of the portfolio of the NSC's Senior Director for European affairs.

This inability to locate Central Asia in the mental map of U.S. foreign policy, and placing the South Caucasus as a low-level priority in the Europe bureau, have real-world consequences. The most glaring example, perhaps, is in the U.S. approach to China. The Obama Administration famously announced a "Pivot to Asia," focusing on the coming U.S. rivalry with the rising Asian power. But this "pivot" entirely ignored Central Asia, although the region is not only part of Asia but also shares a land border with China. The most recent NSS has a lengthy discussion of China's growing influence in its neighborhood. The document reveals that "across Europe, Asia, the Middle East, Africa, and Latin America, countries are clear-eyed about the nature of the challenges that the PRC poses." But despite Beijing's prominent attention to the region, the drafters of the NSS seemed not to think Central Asia merited inclusion in this regard. Incidentally, this contrasts with the same document's discussion of Russia's threat to neighboring areas, which speaks of the impact on "Europe and Central Asia."

Similarly, the lack of any serious mention of security in the NSS language on Central Asia contrasts brightly with the document's approach to the Middle East. Under that heading, we find that "the United States will support and strengthen partnerships with countries that subscribe to the rules-based international order, and we will make sure those countries can defend themselves against foreign threats."That language would have been very appropriate for Central Asia and the Caucasus, and would have signaled a *real* commitment to their sovereignty and territorial integrity. Alas, it is not to be found.

Conceptual Blindfolds

The NSS is a window into how the U.S. foreign policy establishment sees the world. It is clear that in some areas, the U.S. government tries to adapt to new realities: reflecting this, the concept of the Indo-Pacific finds a place in the 2022 NSS. But it seems that the U.S. national security leadership remains the prisoner of geographic and bureaucratic boundaries that are no longer relevant. Across the large Eurasian continent, in particular, the U.S. has not adapted to a world where divisions into Europe, Asia and Middle East no longer suffice to respond to developments on the ground. The attempt to link Central Asia with South Asia appears to have had moderate success at best in reshaping the mental map of U.S. officials; and at least in the short term, it is undermined in practice by the Taliban takeover of Afghanistan. Meanwhile, it impedes efforts to advance Trans-Caspian transport and trade.

Turkey is another example of a country that does not neatly fit into the U.S. government's geographic bureaus. In spite of its growing role in the Middle East and Central Asia, regions that Turkey has made central to its foreign policy, Turkey is mentioned in a single line under "Europe" but is entirely absent in the Middle East section of the 2022 NSS.

The plain conclusion is that the U.S. national security leadership has proven unable to consistently approach areas that don't fall neatly into decades-old geographic and bureaucratic boundaries. This, perhaps, explains the mind-boggling fact that a strategy focused on Russia and China fails to pay adequate attention to the countries that lie between these powers.

This is unfortunate, given that the document otherwise gets many things right. For example, during both the Bush and Obama Administrations, there was a strong tendency to confuse the normative realm of democracy promotion with the cold realities of geopolitics. For example, in countering Russian imperialism, those two administrations both prioritized the promotion of "emerging democracies" like Georgia, Moldova and Ukraine – while ignoring geopolitically crucial states like Kazakhstan, Uzbekistan and Azerbaijan on account of their lesser commitment to democratic principles. This approach appears to have been replaced by a more fruitful approach: the 2022 NSS correctly identifies the "most pressing strategic challenge" to the U.S. as coming "from powers that layer authoritarian governance with a revisionist foreign policy." It correctly notes that "many non-democracies join the world's democracies in forswearing these behaviors."

Indeed, states in this region fall squarely into the document's definition of "nations that support our vision of a free, open, prosperous, and secure world" – countries that "do not embrace democratic institutions but nevertheless depend upon and support a rules-based international system." Encouragingly, the document aspires to "support every country, regardless of size or strength, in exercising the freedom to make choices that serve their interests." But with current conceptual blindfolds, the U.S. government is tying its hands behind its back when it comes to Central Asia and the Caucasus.

Conclusion

America's inability to place Central Asia in its strategic map of the world is no longer tenable. Even before the withdrawal from Afghanistan, it was clear that the region had come to be viewed solely through the lens of America's presence in that country, and that this was no longer adequate. Two years after the withdrawal, little has been done to retool America's approach to the region. It will no longer do for the State Department and NSC to draw different maps of Eurasia, which lead a crucial emerging world region to fall between the cracks. A deeper rethink of America's mental map of the Eurasian continent is long overdue.

Azerbaijan's Strategic Patience in a Changing World

Anar Valiyev and Inara Yagubova

For the last 30 years Azerbaijan has aimed to restore its territorial integrity and political independence through its multi vector foreign policy, avoiding joining any military blocks or unions. In line with its multi–vector foreign policy, amid geopolitical changes in the region, Azerbaijan's foreign policy is based on a "strategic patience" approach which enables it to delicately balance between the collective West and Russia. Meanwhile, with the geopolitical tectonic changes due to Ukrainian crisis, Baku is utilizing its energy resources and transit potential to secure itself against regional powers.

Azerbaijan's foreign policy since independence has been focused mainly on three areas. First, the country was keen on restoring sovereignty over regions occupied by Armenia through negotiations and build long-term sustainable peace. The second priority was to preserve political independence from neighboring countries without joining any unions or blocks. Finally, the third priority was economic development through the development of oil reserves and investments in infrastructure projects to make

Azerbaijan a transportation hub. In the question of Karabakh conflict, Azerbaijan used a *strategic patience* approach that reflected a belief that the current *status quo* and occupation is less than ideal, but it is better than many possible consequences of taking action, especially given Moscow's support for Armenia. Meanwhile, Baku was patiently waiting for the geopolitical changes that would allow the country to solve the question of occupation. Beyond that, Azerbaijan also successfully utilized energy agreements with Europe to secure itself against regional powers and gain economic and political independence. Over the last decade, Azerbaijan has invested billions of dollars into commercial infrastructure and transportation projects.

During the last two years, several events significantly impacted Azerbaijan's main priorities of Azerbaijan. First, due to the COVID-19 pandemic the global economy shrunk, bringing new challenges for the country. In response, Baku intensified its efforts to diversify the economy and strengthen its resilience to external shock. The second significant event was the victorious Second Karabakh War (also known as the 44-day war). In its aftermath, Baku is faced with several challenges including dealing with remaining Armenian separatists in the Karabakh region, the presence of Russian peacekeepers, and convincing Armenian authorities to sign a long-awaited peace treaty. As new situations arise that shift the regional geopolitical balance, including Russia's invasion of Ukraine, Azerbaijan relies on a strategy of "silent diplomacy." This involves making numerous deals and partnerships with various power centers through negotiations, avoiding confrontation. A key part of this strategy was the signing of the Shusha Declaration with Turkey, opening new era of partnership between Baku and Ankara. The Russia-Azerbaijan declaration on strategic alliance signed in February 2022 in a sense complemented Baku's multi-vector diplomacy. The July 2022 agreement between Azerbaijan and the European Union on increasing gas supplies to Europe was another important milestone for the country, in effect completing a trifecta of agreements.

Regional Processes and Implications for Azerbaijani Security Policy

Since the 2008 Russian-Georgian war, when Moscow began to behave more assertively in the South Caucasus, Baku tried to build good relations with Russia, hoping to get Kremlin's support in resolving the Karabakh conflict. In contrast, Baku did not seek deepening relations with the EU or NATO in order not to irritate Russia and increase tensions. Still, Azerbaijan continued to participate in NATO partnership mechanisms and pursued military cooperation with individual NATO member states. Meanwhile, during the Trump administration, the United States minimized its presence in the region. U.S. disengagement from Iraq and Afghanistan also affected Azerbaijan and Baku lost its strategic value for the United States as a major transportation hub for the U.S. Army. At the same time Baku kept its distance from Russian-led organizations like the Eurasian Union and the CSTO and rejected Moscow's attempts to bring Azerbaijan into these organizations.

In 2019, Azerbaijan became Chair of the Non-Alignment Movement – a showcase of its neutrality in the midst of an increasingly dangerous confrontation between the West and Russia. In particular, the relevance of non-alignment as a cornerstone of Azerbaijan's foreign and security policy increased after the Russia–Georgia war of 2008.[1] To some experts, Azerbaijan's NAM membership was intended to reassure Moscow of its lack of ambitions for NATO membership in the aftermath of the 2008 War in Georgia. Others interpret it as a signal to the U.S. and Western governments of a conscious change in Baku's foreign policy direction due to the perceived lack of Western efforts to resolve the Karabakh conflict.[2]

The Second Karabakh war has created new realities in the region. As a result of the war, Azerbaijan elevated relations with Turkey to the alliance level, culminating with the signing of the Shusha Declaration on June 15, 2021. The presence of Turkish military servicemen in the Joint Peacekeeping Monitoring Center, established by the trilateral declaration, strengthened Turkey's position in the region and its influence stabilized the overall security architecture of the South Caucasus. A strong Turkish presence in the South Caucasus is absolutely vital for Azerbaijan in order to balance Russia's increased influence through its peacekeepers in Karabakh.

With its southern neighbor Iran, which is ruled by Shiite clerics, tensions have occasionally flared in the past 30 years. With the eruption of second Karabakh war, Azerbaijan has regularly accused Iran of sending weapons to Armenians in Karabakh. Another, related, factor that recently flamed tensions between two is Azerbaijan's warm ties and active military cooperation with Israel. Another source of tensions between two is Azerbaijan's

---

1   Ilgar Gurbanov, "Relevance of Non-Alignment for Azerbaijan's Foreign and Security Policy," *Caucasus Strategic Perspectives*, vol. 1 no. 1, 2020, pp. 9-19. (https://cspjournal.az/uploads/files/Vol_1_Is_1_Summer2020/2_%20Ilgar%20Gurbanov.pdf)

2   Jason Strakes, "Azerbaijan and the Non-Aligned Movement: Institutionalizing the 'Balanced Foreign Policy' Doctrine," Instituto Affari Internazionali Working Paper 15, May 2015. (https://www.jstor.org/stable/resrep09666#metadata_info_tab_contents)

will to create Zangazur corridor, which will connect two parts of Azerbaijan by land - the Nakhchivan Autonomous Republic and the rest of the country - would cut off Iran's access to Armenia. Tensions further increased in January when a gunman attacked Azerbaijan's embassy in Tehran. Iran views Turkish strong presence in the region as a barrier to its influence in Azerbaijan and fears it threatens to shift the regional balance away from Iran and Russia, especially regarding control of regional transportation infrastructure.

The Russian invasion of Ukraine changed the security paradigm for Azerbaijan, creating a new perception of threat coming from the North. While Azerbaijan's active foreign policy has not changed much in response to the conflict in Ukraine, the Russian invasion brought new challenges to regional stability. President Aliyev, the main influence on the opinion of Azerbaijani elites regarding the conflict in Ukraine, has strongly supported Ukraine's position calling on Kiev to not accept the occupation of its territories. He also condemned what he sees as "Western pacification", the policy of the collective West to accept the occupation of the territories. President Aliyev termed such a policy "wrong" and called on Ukrainians to rely on their own forces and not depend on outside support.[3] A large majority of Azerbaijani society took a pro-Ukraine approach in this crisis, associating it with the occupation of its own territories by a foreign occupant. Russia's occupation of Donbas and other territories is not only seen in parallel with the Armenian occupation of Karabakh but also with "Black January," the Soviet military operation in the streets of Baku of January 19-20, 1990, which aimed to crush

---

3   "President Ilham Aliyev Shares Formula for Azerbaijan's Successful Battle to Restore its Tterritorial Integrity," Trend, April 30, 2022. (https://en.trend.az/azerbaijan/politics/3589675.html)

the independence movement in Azerbaijan. Azerbaijani society associates Russian troops entering foreign lands with their own experiences in Baku and Karabakh. For his part, Hikmet Hajiyev, Foreign Policy Advisor to the President of Azerbaijan, stated that the Russia-Ukraine war was a source of concern, and that Azerbaijan supports a "diplomatic solution" to the conflict within the norms and principles of international law.

So far, local experts and Azerbaijani mass media praise the Azerbaijani government's foreign policy during the conflict. Azerbaijan has sent 380 tons of humanitarian aid worth more than 5.5 million euros to Ukraine, while Azerbaijani state oil company continuously supplying emergency vehicles in Ukraine with the free oil and oil products. But Baku did not join sanctions against Russia. However, when examining Azerbaijan's gains from this calculated balancing and the current state of its bilateral relations, it is less clear that this policy has been effective so far. Harsh rhetoric against Azerbaijan in Russian media and among Russian officials indicates a downward slope in relations between Azerbaijan and Russia. While Moscow hesitates to strain ties with Baku amid the looming chaos in Ukraine, it perceives Baku's independent moves as a challenge to its cause in Ukraine and in the wider neighborhood and therefore sees Azerbaijan as its opposition in the zero-sum conflict between Russia and the West.

The broader concern for Azerbaijan's foreign policy is that the Russia-Ukraine war will have a particularly negative impact on the post-conflict situation in Karabakh. Moscow may try to maximize its hard power through its peacekeepers and seek to put Azerbaijani foreign policy in a framework which serves its foreign policy goals in South Caucasus. If other countries deepen their sanctions against Russia or if the war results in a negative outcome for Moscow, this could impact Russian policies in the region in an unpredictable way and could make the post-conflict environment vulnerable and fragile. Depending on Azerbaijan's actions, Russia could sporadically create a situation in which pro-Russian Armenian separatists will be haunting Azerbaijan and threatening stability in the region, while also seeking to sabotage efforts to bring about a negotiated solution. Another serious consequence of Russia's invasion of Ukraine could be the marginalization and delegitimization of its peacekeeping role in Karabakh. However, the conflict could also be an opportunity for Baku to maximize its positions in Karabakh while Russia is busy with the war in Ukraine.

Consequently, the Russian invasion created a huge domain of uncertainty and increased the need for stability. The invasion has seriously affected and will continue to affect the calculations of decision-makers in Baku as they update their policies towards Moscow and all other stakeholders in response to these significant developments. Therefore, the perception is that the invasion will be a reset point for Azerbaijan's foreign policy, though how it will change will ultimately depend on the war's outcome. If Russia can subdue Ukraine to its terms and come out as winner from this war, then Moscow will become more assertive in the South Caucasus. In case Russia gets weaker, Azerbaijan must be prepared for the possibility of greater decentralization and instability in the North Caucasus, as well as sporadic and unpredictable Russian actions.

Regional Balancing through Economic Policy

Since 2009, cooperation with the EU on bilateral and multilateral formats has become one of Azerbaijan's foreign policy priorities. The EU is Azerbaijan's biggest export and second-biggest import market, with a 51% share of Azerbaijan's exports and a 16% share of Azerbaijan's imports as of 2022. In recent months the Head of the European Council, Charles Michel, hosted the Azerbaijani President and Armenian Prime minister three times, bringing the sides together with the aim of facilitating a peace agreement. The EU has made a €2 billion financial package pledge to Baku within the economic investment plan that is widely regarded as a prelude for deepening partnership between Brussels and Baku and increasing the EU's influence in the region. Building a strategic partnership with the EU serves Azerbaijan's economic goals as well as political strategy to counterbalance Russia in resolving the Karabakh conflict.

Furthermore, the Ukrainian crisis and natural gas supply interruption renewed EU interest in Azerbaijan's energy resources and increased the country's role as a global energy supplier tremendously. In July 2022, Commission President Ursula von der Leyen and President Ilham Aliyev signed the new Memorandum of Understanding on a Strategic Partnership in the Field of Energy which includes a commitment to double the capacity of the Southern Gas Corridor to deliver at least 20 billion cubic metres to the EU annually by 2027. Azerbaijan's oil and gas reserves remain one of the most effective instruments at its disposal to increase its international influence as a main actor in the region. The country can double natural gas exports to Europe within five years and will be able to get into markets that were previously restricted.

The war also had an impact on relations between Azerbaijan and Central Asian states, as the interruptions in the pipeline operations via Russian territory increased the significance of the Trans-Caspian International Transportation Route (TITR) (also known as the Middle Corridor). Kazakhstan's crude oil and oil products are transported via the Caspian Sea and Azerbaijan to Black Sea terminals. Also, the transit potential of TITR will be exploited for cargo flows from Central Asia to the EU via Azerbaijan. The economic and political relations between Azerbaijan and Central Asian states likely will expand amid concerns of Central Asian states, particularly Kazakhstan and Turkmenistan, in diversifying pipeline routes. Furthermore, through the expansion of the Alat port, Azerbaijan aims to build a major trading hub that connects Europe and Asia. Shipping between Alat and Kazakhstan's Aqtau Port is a little under 300 nautical miles and takes just over 24 hours.[4] One of the major projects being implemented by the Azerbaijan and Kazakhstan is the passing of a fiber optic communication line along the bottom of the Caspian Sea. During President Ilham Aliyev's visit to Kazakhstan in April 2023, parties have agreed to leverage the full capacity of the TITR. Hence, in the upcoming years a key focus of Azerbaijan's foreign policy will be expanding trade links with Central Asia, something that will further increase Azerbaijan's role as a transit country in the region.

For Azerbaijan, China today is the new superpower that can invest much-needed funds into infrastructure projects and can counterbalance the influence of Russia. For the last decade, the absence of the United States in the South Caucasus and the EU's relatively passive reaction to the conflicts in the region has opened space for greater Chinese involvement through regional commerce, trade, and infrastructure projects. When China's Belt and Road Initiative (BRI, known until 2016 as One Belt, One

---

4   Chris Devonshire-Ellis, "Caspian Developing as Maritime, Haulage & Rail Hub Between Europe & Asia," *Silk Road Briefing*, August 6, 2020. (https://www.silkroadbriefing.com/news/2020/08/06/caspian-developing-as-maritime-haulage-rail-hub-between-europe-asia/)

Road) project was introduced in 2013 Azerbaijan welcomed the idea and viewed it as an opportunity to catch a share of the transportation benefits. Azerbaijan perceives BRI, and Chinese influence in the region overall, to strengthen ties between Asia and Europe. As China is very far from the South Caucasus, it does not have a political agenda, instead its agenda is purely economic, and therefore Azerbaijan sees China as a reliable partner. China invested $800 million into Azerbaijan's economy and there are more than a hundred companies with Chinese capital in Azerbaijan. The pandemic slowed Chinese penetration in the region, but it is still expected that transportation projects will become the main priority for China in the region. This would benefit Azerbaijan's strategic aim of becoming the transportation and economic hub of the region. All these policies work toward the eventual goal of making Azerbaijan an important geographic location whose independence and sovereignty would be dangerous for anyone to violate since that would meet opposition from other players with a vested interest in Azerbaijan.

Conclusion

Azerbaijan is likely, for the foreseeable future, to continue its policy of "strategic patience". The country will maximize its position based on the circumstances resulting from the Ukrainian crisis. Baku will continue to supply much-needed oil and gas to Europe and will even increase the share that it exports to Europe. Baku will also continue to deepen economic and cultural relations with the EU, possibly even signing a Strategic Partnership with the EU. In the upcoming years strategic energy partnership and partnership on transportation projects with the EU will remain major focuses of Azerbaijani foreign policy. However, political relations with the

EU may remain on the same level as it is today. Additionally, the country is unlikely to deepen relations with NATO, fearing worsening relations with Russia. Instead, Baku will seek to increase its military, economic and political relations with Turkey, harmonizing its military system with the Turkish one, buying weapons from Ankara, and accelerating political relations. Strategic partnerships with Ankara and Tel Aviv are an important part of Azerbaijan's strategy to counterbalance Iranian and Russian influence in the region. Finally, Azerbaijan is likely to seek stability in its relations with Russia. Baku will not seek to join any Russian-led unions but will similarly refrain from supporting anti-Russian sanctions or moves. The presence of Russian peacekeepers gives Moscow an undeniable opportunity to manipulate and maximize its influence and power in the region and this continues to be a major challenge for Azerbaijani foreign policy. In the Karabakh issue, Baku will continue its reconstruction efforts slowly absorbing the territories that are currently under the Russian peacekeepers control, and further developing economic and political ties with Armenia.

In all cases, Baku will refrain from making sporadic or volatile moves, continuing its 28-year "strategic patience" approach.

Georgian Foreign Policy Strategy in Uncertain Times

Kornely Kakachia

Georgia has struggled to achieve its foreign policy goals of restoring its territorial integrity and achieving Euro-Atlantic integration. In recent years, Georgia's relations with the West have cooled somewhat as a result of Georgia's internal problems, while the Georgian Dream government's normalization policy with Russia has led to an increase in Russian influence in the country. In effect, a pro-Western foreign policy was replaced by a balancing approach between Russia and the West. But Russia's invasion of Ukraine exposed the limits of this having-the-cake-and-eating-it approach, which has led to the question whether the GD government lost its foreign policy compass, at a time when its domestic objective to stay in power clashes with the reforms needed to push for EU membership.

Georgia's foreign policy since independence was focused on two main priorities: First, restoration of territorial integrity and sovereignty, and second, Euro-Atlantic integration. While there has not been much tension between the two goals, the second goal was also considered as means to achieve the first. However, Euro-Atlantic integration goes beyond instrumental logic and includes strong ideational meaning for the Georgian public and political elite. "Returning to the European family" has been a significant part of the mythos of Georgia's national identity – which even predates territorial conflicts in Georgia and conflictual relations with Russia.

On the other hand, Russia has been perceived as the main threat to Georgia's sovereignty and national security. Russia's geopolitical dominance in the South Caucasus and the Black Sea region are viewed as an obstacle to Georgia's foreign policy objectives, including Euro-Atlantic integration. Russia as a veto actor is considered to be the main reason behind the stagnation of process of Georgia's NATO integration and the reluctance of the Western partners to engage more with Georgia in areas of security and military cooperation.[1]

Georgian Foreign Policy Priorities in the Last Five Years

Over the last five years Georgia's foreign policy formally remained unchanged aiming at European integration and the development of closer relations with NATO and the United States. Georgia recently submitted a formal application for EU membership, thus entering into a new chapter of internal development strongly driven by public opinion: "irreversible Europeanization." Russia's invasion of Ukraine has opened a window of opportunity for Tbilisi, and has made the achievement of candidate status with the EU more likely. However, unlike Ukraine and Moldova, Georgia

---

1   Kornely Kakachia, Bidzina Lebanidze, and Shalva Dzebisashvili, "Game of (open) Doors: NATO-Georgian Relations and Challenges for Sustainable Partnership," Policy Paper no.18, Georgian Institute of Politics, September 2020. https://gip.ge/publication-post/game-of-open-doors-nato-georgian-relations-and-challenges-for-sustainable-partnership/

has not been able to take full advantage of this chance. Taking into account the recent democratic backsliding in Georgia and the sharp decrease in trust towards the Georgian government, the EU refrained from granting the status of candidate to the country and posed additional conditions for Tbilisi to qualify for this status. However, in a historic decision, the EU recognized Georgia's European perspective and gave the green light to its membership perspective. Despite this, the decision of the European Council was perceived by many as a missed opportunity. This perception is rooted in the fact that Georgia used to be a frontrunner in the Eastern Partnership project, but it is now one step behind the rest of the "Associated Trio."[2] It remains to be seen how the Georgian government will manage to fulfil the 12 recommendations to catch up with Ukraine and Moldova to get EU candidate status.

Against this background, Georgia's relations with the West have somewhat cooled down due to continued problems with Georgia's democratization and good governance. Lack of progress in key areas of democracy and rule of law (such as stagnation of reforms in justice system) have been criticized by the West[3] and the EU even started resorting to democratic conditionality again,[4] for example freezing macro-financial assistance to Georgia in 2021.[5]

At the same time, however, the Georgian Dream (GD) government continued its attempts to normalize relations with Russia. As a result of GD's normalization policy, Georgia again became

---

2 Vano Chkhikvadze, "Georgia's Road to the European Union – Can the Country Catch a Train that has Left the Station," Perspective. Georgian Institute of Politics. July 26, 2022. https://gip.ge/sakartve-los-gza-evrokavshirisken-daeweva-qveyana-dazrul-matarebels/

3 "EU Slams Top Court Appointments in Georgia," Civil.ge, December 2, 2021. https://civil.ge/archives/459326

4 European Parliament, "Georgia: Leading MEPs react to the refusal of the political parties to reach an agreement" April 1, 2021. https://www.europarl.europa.eu/news/en/press-room/20210401IPR01301/georgia-leading-meps-react-to-the-refusal-of-the-parties-to-reach-an-agreement

5 Tornike Mandaria, "Georgia turns down 75 million euros from the EU," *Eurasianet,* September 1, 2021. https://eurasianet.org/georgia-turns-down-75-million-euros-from-the-eu

dependent on Russian imports and exports and the role of Russia increased in many strategic sectors of the Georgian economy, such as tourism and agriculture.[6] The Georgian government also adopted an approach of strategic patience towards Russia. The GD kept a low profile in foreign policy issues that have been important to Russia and has attempted not to irritate its bigger neighbor. This has been the case especially with the Russia-Ukraine war when the Georgian government has kept equidistance between Kyiv and Moscow, did not embrace Western sanctions, and avoided loud criticism of Russia's actions.[7] The GD's Russia-accommodating policy resulted in societal backlashes and domestic political crises in 2019 and 2022. It seems that while the Georgian public is in favor of improving economic relations and people-to-people contacts with Russia, it is strongly against political rapprochement with Russia and the Russia-accommodating policy of the Georgian government.[8]

In sum, while formally there have been no changes in priorities of Georgia's foreign policy, the Georgian government's Russia-accommodating policy and the government's recent and unprecedented anti-western campaign targeting its international partners[9] resulted in informal tectonic changes and a *de facto* reintroduction of the Russian factor in Georgia's foreign policy decision-making process. It seems that pro-Western foreign policy

---

6   Transparency International Georgia. "Georgia's economic dependence on Russia: Trade, tourism, remittances, and Russian companies in Georgia," March 10, 2021. https://www.transparency.ge/en/post/georgias-economic-dependence-russia-trade-tourism-remittances-and-russian-companies-georgia

7   Nini Gabritchidze, "Amid war, bitter exchanges continue to spoil Tbilisi-Kyiv relations," *Eurasianet*, May 4, 2022. https://eurasianet.org/amid-war-bitter-exchanges-continue-to-spoil-tbilisi-kyiv-relations

8   OC Media, "Georgians want their government to support Ukraine" March 15, 2022. https://oc-media.org/features/datablog-georgians-want-their-government-to-support-ukraine/

9   Nini Gabritchidze, "Georgian ruling party intensifies attacks against U.S., EU ambassadors," *Eurasianet*, July 25, 2022. https://eurasianet.org/georgian-ruling-party-intensifies-attacks-against-us-eu-ambassadors

was replaced by a balancing approach between Russia and the West which still favors the West but acknowledges a need to accommodate Russian interests and concerns.

Georgian Foreign Policy Perceptions amid Ongoing Geopolitical Shifts in the Region

The current Georgian government sees Russia as an indispensable power in the region and defines its own role accordingly – as a small state which needs to accommodate the main regional hegemon which also happens to be the main source of danger. The Georgian Dream government seems to view the geopolitical shifts prior to Russia-Ukraine war as confirming Russia's geopolitical dominance in the region. While Euro-Atlantic integration is still Georgia's ultimate goal, GD perceives Western actors as lacking the political will and capacity to provide Georgia with security guarantees against Russia.

The GD's changed approach towards Russia from balancing towards accommodation led to a certain schism regarding the foreign policy perceptions within political elites of Georgia. Unlike the Georgian Dream government, the former ruling party (and now the biggest opposition party) United National Movement (UNM) as well as much of the mainstream opposition parties are opposed to the government's cuddly approach towards Russia. Hence, while there seems to be a consensus among the political elite about the irreversibility of Georgia's pro-Western foreign policy, the consensus falls apart on the question how to deal with Russia. This has been the main reason why the Georgian parliament failed to adopt a cross-party resolution in support of Ukraine amid the Russia-Ukraine war.[10] At the same time, the

---

10 Civil.ge "Georgian Parliament Adopts Resolution Supporting Ukraine, Omits 'Russian Aggression'". February 01, 2022. https://civil.ge/archives/470322

main foreign policy direction – integration with Euro-Atlantic structures – remains unchanged and is shared by a majority of foreign policy elite. However, the extent to which the two vectors (Russia-accommodating posturing and pro-Western foreign policy) are compatible remains to be seen.

Georgia's Regional Focus and Priorities

Georgia's goal of having closer ties with the West, as well as the country's need to maintain balanced relations with its neighbors, are among the factors influencing Georgia's regional foreign and security policy. Georgia is a small country with a compromised security environment and underdeveloped economy. While Georgia's foreign policy has been security-driven due to the presence of territorial conflicts and the occupation of its territory, the country was also looking for beneficial economic ties with external actors to push for its economic development. Georgia's relations with Russia were always torn between Russia's negative impact on Georgia's security and Moscow's economic attraction. Georgia's economic relations with Russia hit their lowest point in 2005-2007 when Russia step by step imposed a full-scale economic and transport embargo on Georgia and economic activities between two countries ground to a halt.[11] Georgia tried to diversify its exports from the lost Russian market. Deteriorating economic and societal ties to Russia were accompanied by increasing ties with the EU and as a result the EU became Georgia's top trade partner. Nevertheless, the GD government that came to power in 2012 decided to reset Georgia's economic and people-to-people

---

11 BBC News "Russia bans Georgia mineral water" May 5, 2006. (http://news.bbc.co.uk/2/hi/europe/4976304.stm)

ties to Russia. As a result, Georgia again became dependent on Russia's market, tourists and strategic goods.[12]

Among other regional actors, Georgia has close strategic partnerships with Turkey and Azerbaijan. The three countries build a significant energy and transport corridor connecting the Caspian Sea and Central Asia to Europe via Turkey and the Black Sea. Turkey is also an important trade partner of Georgia and Azerbaijan is its main source of gas and oil – ensuring Georgia's independence from Russian energy sources. Georgia's relations with Russia's close ally Armenia, by contrast, are relatively modest. The two countries understand each other's foreign policy limitations and nurture pragmatic neighborly relations. Traditionally, Georgia and Ukraine found themselves comrades in both hardship and misfortune. Both still sit outside the European 'zone of democratic peace' — made up mostly of EU and NATO member states — and must therefore adapt their policies to the harsher realities of the former Soviet realm, where power politics dominate. With a tradition of friendly and strategic relations between Tbilisi and Kiev, Georgians followed the Russian invasion in Ukraine with great concern and see the struggle for Ukrainian sovereignty as analogous to their own fate. However, the ambiguous position of present government over the war in Ukraine has strained relations between the two strategic partners.[13] Among non-regional actors, Georgia has the closest economic relations to China. The two countries signed a free trade agreement in 2017 and China has recently become one of Georgia's key trading partners.[14]

---

12 National Statistics Office of Georgia, "External Trade" https://www.geostat.ge/en/modules/catego-ries/35/external-trade
13 Giorgi Lomsadze, "Ukraine recalls ambassador from Georgia," *Eurasianet,* March 1, 2022. (https://eurasianet.org/ukraine-recalls-ambassador-from-georgia)
14 Ibid.

Main Strengths of and Challenges to Georgia's Foreign Policy Approach

Over the first thirty years of independence, Georgia's foreign policy has had several major limitations. First, the key issue was a weak state and the authoritarian tendencies of successive Georgian governments since the country's first president, Zviad Gamsakhurdia. Weak statehood and authoritarian politics made Georgia unattractive and an unpredictable partner for the West and the international community. As Georgia's degree of relations with the EU, NATO and the U.S. increased qualitatively over the years, so the expectations towards Georgia increased. However, successive Georgian governments failed to live up to these expectations. More recently, since signing the Association Agreement with the EU in 2014, the EU and other Western partners expect from Georgia a strong record of good governance and democratic reforms, which the country has not delivered. Neither the UNM government which ruled Georgia from 2003 to 2012 nor the current GD government, in power since 2013, seem to have been ready to conduct genuine democratic and rule of law reforms that would elevate the image of Georgia as a credible and trustworthy partner in increasingly authoritarian and unstable region.

The second weakness has been of an external nature: the presence of Russia as a hostile regional hegemon and, as a result, a hostile external environment. None of the Georgian governments managed to solve this problem. The Russian factor seems also to be a polarizing issue among the Georgian political class, since there is no agreement how to handle it. While the UNM had a more hawkish approach towards Russia, GD decided to appease political Moscow.[15] However, Georgian Dream's cuddly approach to Russia and reluctance to politically side with the West in the Russia-Ukraine conflict may result in Georgia's international isolation and a loss of trust among Georgia's international partners. Therefore, it remains questionable whether GD's Russia-accommodating will be sustainable in the long run and how will it turn out for Georgia.

On the other hand, Georgia's main strength has always been the image of a progressive outpost in an otherwise authoritarian and volatile region. While not a perfect democracy, Georgia has been a frontrunner in areas of good governance reforms and in terms of certain democratic credentials (such as having a vibrant civil society and a more advanced democratic culture compared to many countries in the region). Recently this image has been somewhat tarnished however due to the high level of societal polarization and the political immaturity of major political actors. If Georgia can rebound from the recent crisis and strengthen its image as a progressive force in the region, it can significantly boost its foreign policy niche and make itself a valuable partner for the West.

The Way Ahead in Uncertain Times

As a frontline state in the "gray zone" outside the safety of NATO's security umbrella, Georgia faces the daunting tasks of pursuing Euro-Atlantic integration, strengthening its democratic resilience, preserving sovereignty, and avoiding Russian aggression at the

---

15   Kornely Kakachia, Salome Minesashvili and Levan Kakhishvili, "Change and Continuity in the Foreign Policies of Small States: Elite Perceptions and Georgia's Foreign Policy Towards Russia," *Europe-Asia Studies*, vol. 70 no. 5, 2018, pp. 814-831.

same time.[16] Amid these challenges, the Georgian government is likely to face two dilemmas in the near future. The first dilemma is of a geopolitical nature: how to strike a balance between its Russia-accommodating approach and Euro-Atlantic integration attempts. Russia's invasion of Ukraine exposed the limits of this having-the-cake-and-eating-it approach. While it is understandable and prudent to have a cautious and somewhat predictable policy towards Russia, the GD government seems to have lost its foreign policy compass during its attempts to appease Russia. This puts Georgia in a difficult position due to its transactional foreign and security policy towards Russia. And deliberately or not, by improving economic ties with Russia, Georgian Dream did end up moving Georgia closer to its erstwhile enemy. Against the backdrop of the ruling party's increasing anti-Western rhetoric, there is a possibility that this may further stall Georgia's European integration and increase emerging authoritarianism amid the upcoming 2024 parliamentary elections. Although Georgian benefit from better economic ties with Russia, pursuing closer political relations has proved unpopular among the Georgian public. Despite the GD's rhetoric, existing occupied territories remain an obstacle to improving relations with the Kremlin. Opinion polls repeatedly show that the majority of Georgians perceive Russia as a threat and support the country's pro-European foreign policy.[17] Hence, the Georgian government might continue its balancing act, which in reality looks more like band-wagoning by stealth [18]sort of appeasement policy towards Russia.

---

16   Kakachia Kornely and Shota Kakabadze, "Creeping Finlandization or Prudent Foreign Policy? Georgia's Strategic Challenges amid the Ukrainian Crisis," PONARS Eurasia memo. March 28, 2022. (https://www.ponarseurasia.org/creeping-finlandization-or-prudent-foreign-policy-georgias-strategic-challenges-amid-the-ukrainian-crisis/)

17   Civil.ge. Public Attitudes in NDI Survey. February 2, 2023. https://civil.ge/archives/523658

18   Bidzina Lebanidze, Kornely Kakachia, Bandwagoning by stealth? Explaining Georgia's Appeasement Policy on Russia European Security,2023. https://www.tandfonline.com/doi/abs/10.1080/09662839.2023.2166404?src=&journalCode=feus20

GD needs to reassure the international community, and especially its Western partners, that Georgia's commitment to Euro-Atlantic values and European integration remains unchanged.

Related to this is also a second dilemma: the conflictual interplay between the domestic objectives of the ruling party to keep itself in power and Georgia's main foreign policy objective of European integration and EU membership. Georgia's EU membership prospects, which finally were put on the EU's agenda due to Russia's invasion of Ukraine, will certainly depend on the Georgian government delivering democratic and rule of law reforms. As Georgia needs to accelerate its Europeanization and democratic transformation, ruling regimes in Georgia were generally reluctant to conduct reforms that would endanger their stay in power. If this trend continues it may further strengthen the cooling of relations between the West and Georgia. The current government will need to break this cycle if it wants to pave the way for Georgia's eventual EU membership. Specifically, the Georgian political elite and policy makers need to actively work on reverting the recent setbacks in the Georgia-EU relationship. Most importantly, addressing the challenges in its relations with Ukraine as the strategic partnership with Kyiv is going to be decisive for the regional security architecture in making. Georgia also needs to intensify its cooperation with Turkey a NATO member and a large regional military power that has a potential to counterbalance Russian regional dominance. However, it remains to be seen if Ankara with its transactional foreign policy and strained relations with west ready to take that role. To sum up, Georgia's foreign policy trajectory within the next five years will be shaped by how the Georgian government will solve these two dilemmas.

Between Scylla and Charybdis: Kazakhstan's Foreign Policy in Pursuit of a New Equilibrium

Nargis Kassenova[1]

Russia's war in Ukraine has pushed Kazakhstan's foreign policy out of its comfort zone. Geopolitical divisions between Russia and the West are stark, while those between China and the West are growing. The government is working hard to avoid Western secondary sanctions and diversify partnerships and trade routes, while maintaining good relations with Russia. The development of the Trans-Caspian corridor is of particular importance. Central Asian cooperation is also high on the agenda. While addressing immediate challenges, Kazakhstan's policy makers need to think hard what a new foreign policy equilibrium could look like.

Kazakhstan's foreign policy has been remarkably consistent, having two interlinked priorities at its core: maintaining a close relationship with Russia, the former metropol with die-hard imperial instincts, and balancing it by deepening ties with other external actors. Partnerships with China, the United States, the EU

---

1   **Nargis Kassenova** is a Senior Fellow at the Program on Central Asia, Davis Center for Russian and Eurasian Studies, Harvard University.

and European countries, as well as Turkey have been of primary importance. The relationship with China has grown like a magic bean over the past three decades, and now it rivals, if not overtakes, in importance the one with Russia. The approach has worked well for Kazakhstan, helping it to avoid Russia's wrath and damaging actions (for example, by stirring separatist sentiments in northern Kazakhstan). This success was not cost-free, however, as it involved losses and compromises along the way. The tight links between Kazakh and Russian political elites, on the one hand, made cooperation easier, but on the other created other vulnerabilities and blurring of lines between national and narrow interests.

This approach is being challenged by Russia's war in Ukraine and the major geopolitical and geoeconomic shocks it has caused. Given growing divisions and animosities, pleasing both Russia and the West is now impossible. President Tokayev has compared the situation to passing between Scylla and Charybdis.[2] The situation is complicated by the worsening of relations between the West and China.

The Past Five Years (2018-2022)

The continuity of Kazakhstan's foreign policy can be explained by the continuity of the political leadership and political system, and the overall effectiveness of the adopted approach. The change of president in 2019 – the resignation of Nursultan Nazarbayev and first the appointment and then the election of Kassym-Jomart Tokayev to succeed him – did not affect the approach. This is hardly surprising, given the fact that Tokayev was one of the architects and practitioners of the multi-vector foreign policy. There are

---

2   Tokayev's interview with Russian journalist Andrey Kondrashov on the sidelines of the St. Petersburg International Economic Forum, Kazinform.kz, 15 June 2022 (https://www.inform.kz/ru/mezhdu-scil-loy-i-haribdoy-kasym-zhomart-tokaev-o-sankcionnyh-voynah-rossii-i-zapada_a3944695).

no opposition parties or movements to seriously challenge it in parliament or beyond.

While the overall course has remained stable over the past five years, a number of important developments took place that required modifications. The change of president in Uzbekistan did change that country's foreign policy, making it more open to regional cooperation. The positive dynamic resulted in a sequence of four summits of heads of Central Asian states. The first was convened in Nur-Sultan in 2018, and the latest (and fourth) took place in the Kyrgyz resort town of Cholpon-Ata in July 2022. Kazakhstan has always positioned itself a regional leader and could not miss an opportunity to push for more cooperation under the new circumstances.[3]

Kazakhstan's relations with China were affected by the domestic and international pressures mounting in response to the mistreatment of Muslim minorities in neighboring Xinjiang. The country's public opinion reacted negatively to stories of ethnic Kazakhs being rounded up in "re-education camps" along with Uighurs and other Muslim minorities. The issue was raised in the Kazakh parliament, and Ministry of Foreign Affairs representatives had to bring up the complaints in talks with their Chinese counterparts. In January 2019, it was announced that 2,000 ethnic Kazakhs received the permission to leave Xinjiang and move to Kazakhstan.[4]

The government also had a hard time navigating the international scene. In July 2019 it abstained from signing either of two letters prepared by different coalitions of countries and sent to the

---

3   The government also defined Central Asia and Afghanistan as geographic priorities of its Official Development Assistance in 2021-2025.

4   Radio Free Europe Radio Liberty, "Astana Says China Allowing 2,000 Ethnic Kazakhs To Leave Xinjiang", 9 January 2019 (https://www.rferl.org/a/astana-says-china-allowing-ethnic-kazakhs-to-leave-xinjiang/29699823.html).

UN Human Rights Council – one denouncing China's policies in Xinjiang, the other supporting them. Kazakhstan's policymakers were also not thrilled when U.S. Secretary of State Mike Pompeo on his visit to the country in February 2020 lashed out at Beijing for its violations of human rights and warned Kazakhstan to be wary of Russian and Chinese investment and influence.[5] This left a bad taste of being caught in-between great powers.

Nevertheless, China-Kazakhstan bilateral relations have continued to grow and deepen, and the war in Ukraine gives their cooperation another boost. While close ties with Russia have turned into a liability, partnership with China can provide Kazakhstan with much needed moral and practical support. In June 2022 Chinese Foreign Minister Wan Yi visited Nur-Sultan for the Central Asia-China dialogue and bilateral meetings. He had talks with President Tokayev, and among other things discussed the Trans-Caspian transport route (Middle Corridor) connecting China, Central Asia, and the South Caucasus, bypassing Russia. With Foreign Minister Mukhtar Tleuberdi, they agreed to set up new consulates – in Aktobe and Xian, respectively. It was also announced that President Xi is planning a visit to Kazakhstan in fall 2022.[6]

Another factor that changed the context of Kazakhstan's foreign policy was the withdrawal of U.S. troops from Afghanistan and the takeover of the country by the Taliban. Although Kazakhstan is less exposed to negative influences from the south compared to the other Central Asian states, it is worried about

---

5   Navbahor Imamova, "Pompeo, in Central Asia, Seeks to Counter China", Voice of America, 3 February 2020 (https://www.voanews.com/a/south-central-asia_pompeo-central-asia-seeks-counter-china/6183638.html).

6   Eurasianet, «Китай активизирует экономическую экспансию в Центральной Азии» [China activates economic expansion in Central Asia], 13 June 2022 (https://russian.eurasianet.org/китай-активизирует-экономическую-экспансию-в-центральной-азии).

the situation. Similar to their Uzbek colleagues, Kazakhstani policy makers, see no alternative to working with the Taliban to tackle the humanitarian crisis and foster peace in the country. In October 2021 President Tokayev's Special Representative Erzhan Kazykhan led a delegation to Kabul to discuss humanitarian assistance and restoration of trade and economic links.[7]

The U.S. withdrawal from Afghanistan rekindled fears of U.S. disengagement from Central Asia. Since 2001, the region's proximity to Afghanistan underpinned its importance for the United States. The Obama administration's 2010 announcement of an impending withdrawal created initial anxieties that subsided with time. In August 2021 the withdrawal did take place, leaving disarray inside and outside Afghanistan, and the prospect of the U.S. losing interest became more imminent. However, within half a year, Russia's invasion of Ukraine changed the setting again.

Critical Issues and Dilemmas

The developments of the past five years are undoubtedly on the minds of Kazakhstani policy makers trying to understand how to chart a future course under much more challenging circumstances. There is little public debate on foreign policy due to the lack of full-fledged political opposition or an epistemic community in foreign policy matters. However, one can discern a number of critical issues and dilemmas in media publications and social media discussions.

First among these is the question whether Russia is a threat to Kazakhstan's security and territorial integrity. What does Kazakhstan's membership in the Collective Security Treaty

---

7   Akorda.kz, «Казахстанская делегация посетила с рабочим визитом Афганистан» [Kazakhstan's delegation made a working visit to Afghanistan], 18 October 2021 (https://www.akorda.kz/ru/kazahstanskaya-delegaciya-posetila-s-rabochim-vizitom-afganistan-179039).

Organization and Eurasian Economic Union mean under the new circumstances? How can Kazakhstan distance itself from an increasingly toxic Russia without offending it?

Second, how does Kazakhstan deal with the damage arising from the geopolitical split between Russia and the West? Can it maintain and even deepen relations with the West? Third, how does Kazakhstan mitigate disruptions of its trade with Europe via Russia? What are the best trade diversification options? Fourth, who can Kazakhstan lean on? Is Turkey such a key partner? Fifth, does Russia's self-sabotage lead to a stronger position for China in Central Asia and Eurasia, and what are the implications for Kazakhstan? Finally, is deepening of Central Asian cooperation possible, and can it help Kazakhstan weather the storm?

Some of these issues overlap with the questions that Kazakhstan faced at the dawn of its independence. Once again it needs to find a balance of interests of external powers and diversify its trade routes. However, compared with the past, there are important differences in perceptions and discourses. State-building and nation-building processes have been underway for thirty years. The pride in sovereignty is much more pronounced. President Tokayev's statements at the St. Petersburg International Economic Forum, including a reaffirmation of Ukraine's territorial integrity and criticism of verbal attacks on Kazakhstan by Russian politicians and opinion makers, caused elation in Kazakh social media. There is a better awareness of the country's economic interest as part of the national interest. First Deputy Chief of Staff to the President Timur Suleimenov's interview to Euractiv, stating Kazakhstan's willingness to comply with Western sanctions imposed on Russia, was also very well received by the public.[8] There is a clear sense of affinity and solidarity with Ukraine.

The growing national consciousness underpins not only fears of Russia, but of China as well. Protests against long-term rent of land by Chinese companies and calls to stay away from Chinese credits reflect the worries about the implications of growing bilateral cooperation for the independence of the country. Turkey, on the hand, is seen as a friendly and brotherly nation, whose support is needed to balance the two giant neighbors. Kazakhstan's experts and interested public are attentively watching the Turkish active engagement in the South Caucasus and the ways it exercises leverage vis-à-vis Russia.

Current Priorities

While the public foreign policy debate is muted, government actions are energetic, as required by the urgency of the moment. Kazakhstan's policy makers have worked hard to avoid secondary sanctions by the West and diversify trade routes. One of the immediate challenges was dealing with Kazakhstan's branches of three Russian banks (Sberbank, Alfabank, and VTB).[9] Kazakhstan's government received a grace period from the U.S. OFAC to comply with the sanctions. Within six months, Kazakh owners acquired Sberbank and Alfabank. VTB bank continued to operate in the country, despite the sanctions. Another major challenge, even more difficult to tackle, was the export of most of Kazakh oil via Russia. In 2022 the flow of Kazakh oil via the Caspian

8   Georgi Gotev, "Kazakh official: We will not risk being put in the same basket as Russia", Euractiv, 29 March 2022 (https://www.euractiv.com/section/central-asia/interview/kazakh-official-we-will-not-risk-being-placed-in-the-same-basket-as-russia/).

9   Almaz Kumenov, "Sanctioned Russian banks seeking way out of Kazakhstan", Eurasianet, 21 April 2022 (https://eurasianet.org/sanctioned-russian-banks-seeking-way-out-of-kazakhstan).

Pipeline Consortium pipeline was disrupted four times for unexpected reasons, such as equipment damaged by a storm, discovery of unexploded WW2 mines in the port, and deficiencies in documents regulating accidents.[10]

The troubles with oil export and export of other products via Russia pushed Kazakhstan to intensify its efforts to build the trans-Caspian corridor (also referred to as the Middle Corridor). In November Kazakhstan, Azerbaijan, Georgia and Turkey signed the roadmap for the simultaneous removal of bottlenecks and the development of the Middle Corridor for 2022-2027.[11] The initiative is supported by the European Union. It commissioned the European Bank for Reconstruction and Development (EBRD) to carry out a study to identify the most sustainable transport corridors connecting Central Asia with Europe, and to propose actions for their development.[12]

The role of Turkey as a preferred partner has become particularly pronounced. In May President Tokayev visited Ankara, where the two presidents inked a Joint Statement on enhanced strategic partnership. They signed a number of agreements, including on international intermodal transport of goods and on the organization information exchange and facilitation of customs control. The bilateral military cooperation received a boost as well, as the two presidents. agreed to produce Turkey's Anka drone in Kazakhstan and develop military intelligence cooperation.[13]

---

10 Almaz Kumenov, "Kazakh oil exports across Russia interrupted for fourth time this year", Eurasinet, 23 August 2022 (https://eurasianet.org/kazakh-oil-exports-across-russia-interrupted-for-fourth-time-this-year).

11 Astana Times, "Kazakhstan seeks to enhance transit transport potential of Caspian region, Says Kazakh Foreign minister", 28 November 2022 (https://astanatimes.com/2022/11/kazakh-stan-seeks-to-enhance-transit-transport-potential-of-caspian-region-says-kazakh-foreign-minister/).

12 Anton Usov, "EBRD researches sustainable transport connections between Central Asia and Europe", 7 November 2022 (https://www.ebrd.com/news/2022/ebrd-researches-sustainable-trans-port-connections-between-central-asia-and-europe-.html).

13 Joanna Lillis, "In Turkey, Kazakhstan's president talks trade and China transport", Eurasianet, 11 May 2022, (https://eurasianet.org/in-turkey-kazakhstans-president-talks-trade-and-china-transport); Almaz Kumenov, "Kazakhstan seals deal to produce Turkish drones under license", Eurasianet, 13 May 2022 (https://eurasianet.org/kazakhstan-seals-deal-to-produce-turkish-drones-under-license).

In June President Tokayev led a big delegation to Iran. He participated in the online launch ceremony of the first container train from Kazakhstan through Iran to Turkey. The sides agreed to strengthen trade and economic cooperation in transport, logistics, manufacturing, and agriculture. As a sign of improved relations, Kazakhstan introduced a two-week visa-free regime for Iranian citizens.[14] And in July Tokayev visited Saudi Arabia where he invited the kingdom's investments in the precious metals mining, the petrochemical, nuclear energy, and hydrogen industries, and proposed cooperation in the area of space exploration.[15]

While diversifying its economic and political cooperation away from Russia, Kazakhstan tries hard to maintain good relations with its northern neighbor. Cooperation across the board continues, and symbolic tokens of respect are paid. Tokayev was the only respectable political leader who attended the St. Petersburg International Economic Forum in June and spoke along Putin. It is not an easy balancing act, but Kazakhstan's leadership projects a confident and calm image.

Strengths and Weaknesses

The strengths of Kazakhstan's foreign policy have been well recognized. With the help of its multivector, multilateral approach, the country has friendly relations with all its neighbors and beyond, and has embedded itself well in the regional and global orders. Another, less discussed positive feature of the policy is its emphasis on serving the country's citizens. The 2020 Foreign

---

14 Zhanna Shayakhmetova, "Kazakhstan and Iran agree to boost trade and economic cooperation during Tokayev's visit to Iran", 20 June 2022 (https://astanatimes.com/2022/06/kazakhstan-and-iran-agree-to-boost-trade-and-economic-cooperation-during-tokayevs-official-visit-to-tehran/).

15 Forbes Kazakhstan, «Токаев предложил инвесторам Саудовской Аравии разведать в РК более 60 месторождений драгметаллов» [Tokayev proposed to investors of Saudi Arabia to explore in the RK more than 60 deposits of precious metals], 24 July 2022 (https://forbes.kz/process/tokaev_predlo-jil_investoram_saudovskoy_aravii_razvedat_v_rk_bolee_60_mestorojdeniy_dragmetallov/).

Policy Concept notes among its priorities the effective protection of rights, freedoms and legitimate interests of Kazakhstanis. One practical outcome of this approach is the consistency of the government's efforts to evacuate its citizens from dangerous areas.[16] Such an approach is part of the nation-building process.

The weaknesses of the foreign policy during the Nazarbayev era was the excessive investment in vanity projects, such as hosting Congresses of Leaders of World and Traditional Religions and the OSCE summit in Astana, and the aggrandizement of the First President. In November 2021, at the Ministry of Foreign Affairs, Tokayev criticized the lack of inter-agency coordination in the protection of national interests, citing such problems as the shallowing of the Zhayik/Ural river, the delay of Kazakhstani goods on the Chinese border, and the infringement of the interests of Kazakhstan's businesses in neighboring countries. He prioritized the "re-setting" of the economic diplomacy and Central Asian policy.[17]

What Next?

Kazakhstan's foreign policy is currently in overdrive to maintain the geopolitical balance between Russia and the West and perform damage control. Less dramatic but equally profound for Kazakhstan's future is the ongoing "decoupling" between China and the West. Whether it can find a new equilibrium remains to be seen. While the consistent interest of China, the country's next-door neighbor, can be taken for granted, the full-fledged

---

16 Kaztag, "Kazakhstan completes evacuation of its citizens from Ukraine", 30 March 2022 (https://kaz-tag.kz/en/news/kazakhstan-completed-evacuation-of-its-citizens-from-ukraine).

17 Akorda.kz, «Глава государства принял участие в расширенном заседании коллегии МИД» [Head of the state took part in the enlarged session of the MFA collegium], 18 November 2021 (https://www.akorda.kz/ru/glava-gosudarstva-kasym-zhomart-tokaev-prinyal-uchastie-v-rasshirennom-zasedanii-kollegii-mid-18105730).

engagement of the EU and U.S. is less assured, and will require effort on the part of Kazakhstan.

It is clear that the development of the Trans-Caspian corridor and partnerships with the states of South Caucasus, Turkey, and Iran will be a priority over the next several years. Turkey is of particular importance as a brotherly Eurasian power ready to provide Kazakhstan with all kinds of support. There will be efforts to tap more into the potential of the relations with the Gulf countries. They are seen as a source of investments and as power brokers in the global energy sector.

Cooperation with Central Asian states will also be high on the agenda. Kazakhstan's government does not have regional integration aspirations (in Cholpon-Ata President Tokayev proposed the creation of consultative platforms), but it is ready to draw on the new opportunities – primarily, having a like-minded partner in Uzbekistan – and push for change.[18]

---

18 Akorda.kz, "Speech by President Kassym-Jomart Tokayev at the 4ᵗʰ Consultative Meeting of the Heads of States of Central Asia", 21 July 2022 (https://www.akorda.kz/en/speech-by-president-kassym-jomart-tokayev-at-the-fourth-consultative-meeting-of-the-heads-of-states-of-central-asia-216535).

Kyrgyzstan and the Changing Geopolitics of Central Asia

Shairbek Dzhuraev

Throughout its independence, Kyrgyzstan's foreign policy sought to balance developing new external and maintaining good relations with Russia. With the growing geopolitical tension in the broader Eurasian region, such balancing has become increasingly difficult. In the meantime, China and Turkey have become influential foreign partners. Bishkek's relations with the neighboring states remain mostly cooperative, except for Tajikistan. The paper reviews the above trends in the context of the country's ever-dynamic domestic politics and concludes by noting the strengths, weaknesses, and priorities of Kyrgyzstan's foreign relations.

Three characteristics of Kyrgyzstan, a newly independent state as of 1991, determined its foreign policy priorities for years to come. First, it was an economically and militarily small state in its neighborhood, making the pursuit of security relationships the most significant task in international relations. Second, Kyrgyzstan was a resource-poor country, and this turned foreign policy into a quest for securing external aid. Third, as of 1991, Kyrgyzstan was the only Central Asian state where the Soviet-time communist party leadership was in the opposition, not in power, paving the way for more genuine liberalization reforms in the 1990s.

Combined, the three factors above shaped the contours of Kyrgyzstan's international engagement, best described in President Akaev's favorite phrase: "small states need big friends."[1] Russia remained the country's main political and military ally, whose patronage was particularly valued in the context of unfamiliar China and taciturn Uzbekistan. In the meantime, Kyrgyzstan's liberal policies attracted much-needed support from the U.S. and Europe. For most of the 1990s, combining the "Russia first" policy with building relations with the rest of the world caused few problems. Kyrgyzstan's economic and political reforms largely followed those of Russia, where President Yeltsin, like Akaev, enjoyed the backing of the West against their biggest internal rivals, the communists.

Balancing became more difficult as Russia's relations with the West deteriorated in the late 1990s. President Akaev acknowledged the pressure, penning an article for a Russian journal to argue that Kyrgyzstan's special relations with Russia should allow a "corridor of opportunities" to develop relations with "third countries."[2] The color revolutions in 2003-05 and the Russian-Georgian war in 2008 did not leave space for such a corridor. President Kurmanbek Bakiyev, who succeeded Akaev following the 2005 revolt, learned this the hard way when he fell out with Russia over a U.S. airbase shortly before opposition protests toppled him from power in 2010.

---

1   Askar Akaev, 'Speech at the United Nations', 2004 <https://www.un.org/ru/ga/59/plenary/kyrgyz.pdf>.

2   Askar Akaev, "Kuda Idet Tsentral'naya Aziya? (Where is Central Asia Heading?", *Russia in Global Affairs*, no. 4, 2003 (http://www.globalaffairs.ru/number/n_2126).

Recent Changes in Kyrgyzstan's Foreign Policy

For the past 30 years, Kyrgyzstan has maintained a consistent approach to international relations that is typical for smaller nations. The country's foreign policy aims to minimize risks and maximize benefits by adapting to emerging external conditions rather than pursuing a specific agenda. However, the country's external environment has seen significant changes, prompting responses and adjustments from Bishkek. Three topics stand out.

At a broader international level, the growing geopolitical tension in the region exposed the downside of Kyrgyzstan's "big friends" strategy. More specifically, it became evident to Bishkek that the risky situation of "too many competing big friends" could swiftly turn into one of a "no good big friend." Keen to restore credibility in the eyes of Moscow following Bakiev's failed gamble, president Almazbek Atambaev closed the U.S. airbase at Manas in 2014 and canceled the cooperation framework agreement with the U.S. in 2015. The same year, Kyrgyzstan joined the Moscow-initiated Eurasian Economic Union (EAEU). However, Russia's favor, hard-won by severing ties with the United States, proved flimsy. First, Atambaev's rhetoric suggested it was the risks of not joining rather than the benefits of joining that drove the EAEU decision.[3] Second, in 2015, Russia walked away from one of its biggest commitments to President Atambaev, to invest about $3 billion in constructing hydropower plants in Kyrgyzstan.

The Chinese front is another example. Between 2010 and 2017, Beijing's share of Kyrgyzstan's external debt increased from 5.7% to 41.6%, meaning that Kyrgyzstan stopped borrowing

---

3   Pavel Dyatlenko, "Kyrgyzstan Gets Soft Terms for Customs Union Entry," Institute for War and Peace Reporting, June 6, 2014. (https://iwpr.net/global-voices/kyrgyzstan-gets-soft-terms-customs-union-entry).

elsewhere.⁴ However, in 2018, as bells started ringing about China's debt-trap diplomacy, the money flow from Beijing effectively stopped. While many reasons could be cited, an important factor was a 2018 corruption case in Kyrgyzstan in which two prime ministers were jailed for embezzling a $400 million Chinese loan. Although the corruption case was linked to internal political infighting in Bishkek, the case was unwelcome and embarrassing for Beijing's highly publicized Belt and Road Initiative. China's image of a "benevolent neighbor" had also seen cracks in 2016, when China suspended visas to Kyrgyzstan for two years, forcing Kyrgyz to seek Kazakh citizenship to continue business with China. In short, the post-2010 period has shown that the interests and enthusiasm of big friends cannot be taken for granted.

At the regional level, recent years saw two significant changes in Kyrgyzstan's immediate neighborhood. On the positive side, the 2016 political transition in Uzbekistan transformed the latter from the biggest source of trouble for Kyrgyzstan into an amicable neighbor. Under Islam Karimov, Uzbekistan was mostly an unfriendly neighbor. Bilateral relations, particularly concerning borders, water, and energy issues, had remained cool or frozen since the early 2000s. The new Uzbek leader, Shavkat Mirziyoyev, became a relief for Bishkek as he declared a willingness to discuss and resolve any problems with Uzbekistan's neighbors, starting with border delimitation and reopening border crossings. In February 2023, Kyrgyzstan and Uzbekistan completed the border delimitation, something that was appeared unrealistic a few years earlier.

---

4   Azattyk, "Ne otkazyvayet. Kak Kitay za 7 let stal osnovnym kreditorom Kyrgyzstana" (No refusal. How China has become the main creditor of Kyrgyzstan in 7 years), *Azattyk*, September 13, 2018. (https://rus.azattyk.org/a/kyrgyzstan-debt-china/29486035.html)

However, the thaw in relations with Uzbekistan coincided with a dramatic deterioration in Kyrgyzstan's relations with Tajikistan. For most of the post-1991 period, this southern neighbor was a natural ally. Small, poor, and upstream, Kyrgyzstan and Tajikistan had many shared challenges. While the two countries have plenty of border and water disputes, their governments found ways to keep such issues under wraps. However, since the early 2010s, the dynamics have worsened. If issues in the past revolved around summer-time skirmishes over water among border area residents, recent years saw a dramatic militarization of the conflict. The use of heavy weaponry, including mortar shells and grenade launchers, became a norm.[5] In April 2021 and September 2022, large-scale fighting between the two countries resulted in dozens killed and tens of thousands displaced. Kyrgyzstan accused its neighbor of aggression, as several of its border villages had remained under Tajik troops control for days. Bishkek and Dushanbe have since resumed bilateral talks on border delimitation, yet the risk of military escalation remains high.

New Pressures for New Leaders: Afghanistan and Ukraine

In October 2020, post-electoral protests forced the sitting president Sooronbay Jeenbekov to vacate his post. The new leader, Sadyr Japarov, announced major changes, from reinstating a strong presidential system to reclaiming national ownership over Kumtor, the country's largest gold mine. The latter, combined with his ability to use social media, earned Japarov a reputation as a nationalist and populist. However, as dramatic events unfolded

---

5   Timur Toktonaliev, Lola Olimova, and Nazarali Pirnazarov, "Kyrgyz-Tajik Row After Border Clash," Institute for War and Peace Reporting, January 15, 2014.(https://iwpr.net/global-voices/kyrgyz-tajik-row-after-border-clash).

in Afghanistan and Ukraine, Kyrgyzstan's new president proved no different from his predecessors, staying true to the strategy of minimizing risks and sticking to the crowd.

The collapse of the Afghan government In August 2021 was a more straightforward case. Kyrgyzstan does not border Afghanistan and has thus been spared the need for precautionary military preparations. Kyrgyzstan's biggest issue with Afghanistan remains the incursions of the Islamic Movement of Uzbekistan (IMU) fighters back in 1999 and 2000, during the Taliban's previous spell in Kabul. The risk of Afghanistan becoming a safe haven for Central Asian militants remains. However, like most Central Asian states, Kyrgyzstan has decided that rejecting the Taliban is unlikely to help. Drug trafficking is routinely mentioned in Central Asia's relations with Afghanistan. However, it is unclear whether Central Asian governments see this as a problem or whether the Taliban would make a difference.

As Afghan towns started falling to the Taliban in the summer of 2021, Sadyr Japarov appointed Talatbek Masadykov, a regional security expert with experience in the UN missions, as deputy chairman of the country's security council. The move aimed to fill the competence gap in the government on regional security issues. As dramatic events unfolded in August 2021, Bishkek took a reserved stance, joining its neighbors Kazakhstan and Uzbekistan in establishing informal contacts with the Taliban and avoiding conflict-prone rhetoric. Tajikistan has taken a more belligerent stance towards the Taliban, with the Central Asian governments appearing to have "agreed to disagree" on this topic.

Russia's Ukraine aggression in February 2022 posed a much bigger challenge. For many reasons, Bishkek could not afford to express support for Ukraine. Kyrgyzstan's multi-level dependence on Russia and a web of formal and informal connections make it one of Russia's few allies. It is part of Russia-led security and economic alliances (CSTO and EAEU), and remittances from Kyrgyz labor migrants in Russia make up about one-third of the country's GDP. Further, the Kyrgyz elite is well aware of Russia's ability to influence the domestic political situation in Kyrgyzstan and, thus, does not see alienating Russia as an option.

At the same time, like other Central Asian states, Kyrgyzstan is concerned about Russia's aggression. For all Moscow's talk about the threat of NATO or "de-Nazification," Ukraine is, first of all, a fellow former Soviet republic whose right to existence Russian leaders have denied. This does not bode well for Central Asian states, none of which existed in their present shape before 1991. Russia's Putin had spoken on this more than once, most recently on June 17, 2022, when he called the territory of the Soviet Union "historic Russian lands." Furthermore, the unprecedented U.S. and European sanctions against Russia and the uncertainty of scenarios for the end of the war make taking a position a precarious venture.

In light of the above, Kyrgyzstan focused on minimizing the risks. On the eve of the Russian invasion of Ukraine, President Japarov offered, albeit in social media and using convoluted language, an "understanding" of Russia's recognition of Donetsk and Luhansk. As Russia invaded Ukraine, Kyrgyzstan has maintained the language of neutrality, not least helped by similar but more explicit stances of Kazakhstan and Uzbekistan. Also, the Kyrgyz government showed little tolerance for public expressions of support for Russia or Ukraine, going as far as to arrest those who, in its view, misrepresented Kyrgyzstan's position on the subject.[6]

---

6   Azattyk, "Direktor Next TV zaklyuchen pod strazhu na dva mesyatsa," (Next TV director jailed for two months), March 5, 2022. (https://rus.azattyk.org/a/31737444.html).

Priority Partners and Priority Policies

In a recent interview, President Japarov succinctly described his understanding of foreign policy, saying that "[as a] small country, we must have respectful relations with all countries." The statement resonates with both Akaev's references to the country's size and scholars' description of Kyrgyz foreign policy as a "policy of non-contradiction and friendly relations with all".[7] In practice, the list of Kyrgyzstan's foreign partners is short. Lists often start with Russia and the states of Central Asia and include all or some of China, the U.S., the EU, and Turkey. Despite being short, the list does not allow neat mapping along with policy priorities.

Russia remains the primary foreign policy partner for at least three reasons. First, it is the biggest trade partner for Kyrgyzstan, particularly as a) the primary destination for Kyrgyzstan's exports other than gold, b) the single supplier of gasoline and natural gas to Kyrgyzstan, and c) the rule-setter within the Eurasian Economic Union. Second, Russia hosts about one million Kyrgyz labor migrants. Finally, Russia's political clout remains massive, owing to the above-listed economic roles and the solid public support it enjoys in Kyrgyzstan. The latter is critical, allowing Moscow to influence Kyrgyzstan's policies and politics from within. Bishkek's uneasiness with the above has not yet translated into specific measures.

In the early 1990s, post-Soviet Central Asian states appeared to be natural allies, sharing the challenges of unexpected independence. However, today these states make a diverse group. Kazakhstan has long been the closest nation for cultural/linguistic roots but also for its prominent economic role. Large chunks

---

7   Andrew Kuchins, Jeffrey Mankoff, and Oliver Backes, *Central Asia in a Reconnecting Eurasia: Kyrgyzstan's Evolving Foreign Economic and Security Interests*, Lanham: Rowman & Littlefield, 2015, p. 4.

of private business in Kyrgyzstan belong to Kazakh corporations (including two of the three largest mobile operators). But more importantly, the Kyrgyz-Kazakh border is a critical transport bottleneck, controlling the movement of goods to and from Russia, Europe, and Turkey. Although there are other vital issues on the bilateral agenda (such as transboundary water and grain), Kazakhstan's control over transport routes has increasingly posed a policy headache for Bishkek.

The priority accorded to transport diversification has been key to Kyrgyzstan's relations with two other neighboring countries, China and Uzbekistan. In 2022, President Japarov declared that the decades-long project of the China-Kyrgyzstan-Uzbekistan railroad was about to get launched this year. In his words, Kyrgyzstan needed the railroad like "air and water."[8] The railroad would make goods cheaper and relieve the pressure of strong dependence on Kyrgyzstan's northern neighbor. While very attractive, the project is costly, and it remains to be seen whether construction indeed kicks off any soon. That said, China is already one of the biggest economic players for Kyrgyzstan due to the massive trade volume between the two and large-scale loans to the Kyrgyz government. Kyrgyz-Uzbek relations remain relatively small in scope. However, Tashkent's central location for transport routes and openness for widening cooperation make it one of Kyrgyzstan's most attractive foreign policy partners.

Finally, the 2021-22 conflicts at the Kyrgyz-Tajik border transformed Tajikistan into the top external threat and turned military preparedness into a policy priority. Although border disputes are nothing new in the region, the recent clashes set a

---

8   Sadyr Japarov, "Interview to Kabar News Agency," Kabar, May 30, 2022. (http://kg.kabar.kg/news/maga-bailyktyn-keregi-zhok-prezident-sadyr-zhaparovdun-kezektegi-maegi/).

record for being the deadliest and involved, for the first time, occupation of several Kyrgyz border villages by Tajik troops. Now, both countries' leaders refrain from hostile rhetoric. However, with no explicit high-level commitment to the non-use of force and militarization of the border areas, the risk of conflict escalation remains high.

Against the background of border clashes, calls grew in Kyrgyzstan for more security cooperation, with Turkey often singled out as a potential partner. The latter has already stepped up its engagement in Central Asia both on a bilateral basis and through the symbolic transformation of the Cooperation Council of Turkic Speaking States into the Organization of Turkic States. Kyrgyzstan's well-publicized purchase of Turkish drones, following the latest round of military conflicts with Tajikistan, illustrates Ankara's broadening presence in Kyrgyzstan and Central Asia.

Strengths and Weaknesses of Kyrgyzstan's Foreign Policy

There is a relatively stable set of factors that define the basic parameters of Kyrgyzstan's international relations. Kyrgyzstan is not in a zone of active warfare, nor does it face an imminent threat of such, the border disputes with neighbors notwithstanding. The country's size and geography impose important limitations on what can and cannot be pursued internationally. The above, however, does not deprive the country of agency and responsibility for developing the policy approaches most appropriate to maneuver in its external environment. The latter task, in turn, requires a good understanding of the strengths and weaknesses of the country's foreign policy approach.

The single biggest strength of Kyrgyzstan's foreign policy is its commitment to developing relations with all its partners. Although this sounds like a routine description of the foreign policy of any country, in the context of Kyrgyzstan, it is primarily a move away from the "one patron" strategy. The country's external dependence is disproportionately tied to a few foreign policy partners. If such dependence was an acceptable price to pay for overcoming existential insecurity in the early 1990s, today it has become an obstacle to more sustainable development.

Once known as a "multi-vector" foreign policy, the approach to widening the map of international engagement is not free of risk. Politicized comments warning about the risks of "milking two cows" are not uncommon in Kyrgyzstan. Switching to a single cow should not be the only alternative here. Kyrgyzstan's needs in transport corridors, energy supply, and external trade demand diversification. Combined with adequate planning and communication to mitigate risks, the efforts to diversify the country's international partnerships, if sustained, will serve Kyrgyzstan's needs well.

What characteristics of Kyrgyzstan's foreign policy could jeopardize all efforts? This list can be long, but two factors deserve particular mention here. The first is the negative impact of domestic political processes. While not a model democracy, Kyrgyzstan has developed a relatively dynamic political system in which the ruling regimes are chronically insecure. The impact on foreign relations, however, has been detrimental. At various points, both the government and opposition proved to be prone to unnecessary nationalistic rhetoric, only damaging the country's international credibility in the process. Also, using foreign policy jobs to reward

loyal aides or silence loud political critics results in sidelining pro-
fessional diplomats and does not help the country's international
relations.

The second weakness of Kyrgyzstan's foreign policy approach
is its habit of counting on external aid for every priority issue. In
some ways, this is a legacy of the 1990s, when Kyrgyzstan had few
resources. The country's small economy is a known limitation, but
so is the level of corruption that keeps the state's budget thin. Kyrgyzstan's leaders should realize that domestic resource mobiliza-
tion is critical to moving forward with any strategic foreign policy
goal. Relying on the "other side" will only prolong the country's
dependence and vulnerability. There is a growing understanding
of this problem in the country. The 2018 country development
program mentioned the need to move away from the "dependency
approach" ("izhdivencheskiy podkhod"), and more recently, Prime
Minister Akylbek Japarov claimed Kyrgyzstan was "abandoning
the 'poor' country syndrome."⁹ Policy reforms and their outcomes
will demonstrate whether Japarov meant what he said.

Looking Ahead

There is high international volatility in the region and the world.
The dynamics of international relations in Central Asia will significantly depend on developments outside the region, such as the
Russian-Ukrainian war, relations between Russia and the West,
and developments in Afghanistan, to name a few. Under the circumstances, Kyrgyzstan's foreign policy will continue focusing on
mitigating risks at two levels.

First, Kyrgyzstan is likely to take a risk-averse international

---

9   Government of the Kyrgyz Republic, "Akylbek Japarov: My otkazyvayemsya ot sindroma 'bednoy'
    strany," (Akylbek Japarov: We are abandoning the "poor" country syndrome)', 2021 <https://www.
    gov.kg/ru/post/s/20602-akylbek-zhaparov-biz-zhakyr-lk-sindromunan-bash-tartuudabyz> [accessed
    18 June 2022].

stance on increasingly sensitive issues. One priority will be to have Moscow remain content with Bishkek's "impartial" position on Ukraine as well as on Kyrgyzstan's relations with other bigger powers. This task is not easy. Recent talks about Kyrgyzstan and the U.S. signing a new cooperation agreement have caused detailed and critical commentaries in Russian papers. On a different subject, Russia has long resisted the idea of the China-Kyrgyzstan-Uzbekistan railroad. President Japarov confirmed this recently, saying he had convinced Putin of the importance of the project for Kyrgyzstan's needs. Kyrgyzstan's relations with China and Turkey also have "sensitive" aspects that require careful communication and potentially unpopular actions.

Second, addressing Kyrgyzstan's critical economic vulnerabilities will remain a longer-term priority. To the extent it succeeds in finding resources, Kyrgyzstan will move forward with large-scale projects on energy and transport. China and Uzbekistan appear to be strategic actors, offering East to West transport corridors, regardless of progress on the railroad project. An increasingly difficult situation with electricity production means Kyrgyzstan will have to work on expanding production but also look for greater energy trade/transit cooperation with its neighbors, particularly Kazakhstan, Uzbekistan, and Turkmenistan.

The scope and pace of Kyrgyzstan's foreign policy initiatives will also depend on domestic political dynamics. The experience of three regime overthrows in fifteen years means that the specter of a fourth continues to haunt the government, risking turning foreign policy priorities into an element of political squabbling. Addressing this challenge requires a government that is more legitimate, more competent, and less corrupt. In the past, the task repeatedly failed, making the challenge more interesting.

Turkmenistan Lifts Its Head

S. Frederick Starr

In recent months Turkmenistan has emerged from its self-imposed shell. Under its new president, Serdar Berdimuhamedov, it has launched a very active, though still cautious, foreign policy. While reaffirming its neutral status, which the UN recognized in 1995, it has intensified its relations with all the global powers and, significantly, with its neighbors as well. Both the U.S. and EU have applauded these initiatives and the new president's strategic concept that underlies them. However, events unfold, Turkmenistan has decisively lifted its head, and will henceforth be a significant factor in regional and continental affairs and not simply a perplexing outlier.

Many in the outside world have long viewed Turkmenistan as an enigma. Impressed by the country's vast gas resources, they failed to recognize the profound backwardness that was the Soviet legacy in many spheres. Education, public health, business, and technology all lagged, and the main posts were filled by Russians. Formerly divided among nomadic groups, the Turkmen people lacked a clear national identity, which the founding president,

Saparmurat Niyazov, attempted to fill with grand architectural projects and his own idiosyncratic exposition of national values.

A major turning point was reached when Russia's Prime Minister Viktor Chernomyrdin and Chairman of Gazprom Rem Vyakhirev, irked by Turkmenistan's demand to be paid a fair price for its gas, abruptly closed down the country's sole export pipeline in 1997. Ashgabat was right to demand more, for Moscow had been reselling the gas it had bought for pennies to Europe at world prices, pocketing the profit. This move by Moscow caused the Turkmen economy almost to collapse, unheated schools had to be closed, and the country came close to starvation. Turkmenistan's response was adroit and effective: it proposed to Beijing a Turkmenistan-China pipelines that remains today the country's main source of income. Otherwise, Ashgabat pursued policies that isolated the country both economically and culturally. True, it was an active leader of the successful effort by all five former Soviet republics of Central Asia to define their region as a nuclear free zone. But in most respects Turkmenistan pulled back from international engagement in order to pursue an isolationist strategy. Critics in the West pointed to Ashgabat's curtailment of human rights and freedoms but made little effort to address the fragility and backwardness that gave rise to them.

New President, New Regional Priorities

A decisive change occurred eight months ago when President Gurbanguly Berdimuhamedov turned over his office to his forty-year-old son, Serdar. The transition was smooth, and the outgoing president continues to function as head of the Senate and a kind of roaming ambassador on priority projects. But a pronounced change of course became immediately evident. Whereas

Berdimuhamedov Sr. was, and is, a man of diverse and colorful enthusiasms who revels in the details of projects, his son, Serdar, austere and self-effacing, quickly revealed a focus on strategy. In his "state of the union" speech on 23 September he laid out what he considers Turkmenistan's two most urgent needs: to overcome its isolation as a landlocked country through the development of all forms of transport including, of course, pipelines for the transmission of gas; and to open up heretofore underdeveloped channels of communication with the larger world. Inter alia, amidst Russia's war on Ukraine he also pointed to the growing demands of security and called for serious investments in defense. In short, the new government in Ashgabat reconsidered Turkmenistan's long-held isolationist interpretation of its neutral status and replaced it with multi-sided engagement designed to enhance the country's economy and security.

This new approach is evident in Turkmenistan's recent actions at both the regional level within Central Asia and the international level. Within the region Ashgabat has greatly expanded its relations with both Kazakhstan and Azerbaijan – Kazakhstan because it is a potential consumer of Turkmen gas, and Azerbaijan because it is the most promising corridor for Turkmen gas to Europe and because its new Caspian port, Alat, is the vitally important western counterpart to the new Turkmen port of Turkmenbashi. This pairing of interests led President Serdar Berdimuhamedov to convene presidents of the five Caspian littoral states in June 2022. Azerbaijan's national oil company, SOCAR, promptly announced that it would soon open an office in Ashgabat.

For centuries the relationship between the Turkmen tribes and the settled peoples of Bukhara, Khiva and Samarkand could not have been worse. The new era of independence brought further tension between Turkmenistan and Uzbekistan until 2007, when President Gurbanguly Berdimuhamedov launched a policy of cooperation and friendship with Tashkent. For both countries the transport of energy and the promotion of trade and investments were the main drivers. Reflecting this astonishing change, Uzbekistan's president Shavkat Mirziyoyev recently announced during a visit to Ashgabat that he hoped Uzbekistan would soon import Turkmen gas and that the two countries would establish an international trade zone on their border. Shortly thereafter another Uzbek official announced the purchase of up to four billion kilowatt hours of Turkmen electricity.

Building on this opening, Kyrgyzstan's Energy Minister Talaibek Ibrayev announced in late October that he was negotiating to buy 350 billion cubic meters of Turkmen gas and two billion kilowatt hours of electricity. Pricing problems stalled this deal, but Kyrgyzstan meanwhile committed to buy electricity from Uzbekistan generated with Turkmen gas. Meanwhile, Kazakhstan's President Kassym-Jomart Tokayev announced earlier in October that he was seeking to import 1.5 billion cubic meters of gas per year from Turkmenistan and proposed to build a grain storage depot in Turkmenistan to provide wheat to Afghanistan.

None of these sales of gas and electricity are large by global standards, but they indicate Serdar Berdimuhamedov's commitment not only to a more active regional role but also to the development of a solid economic base for these new arrangements. President Berdimuhamedov's dreams of regional communication and connectivity cannot be achieved amidst the mutual wariness and even hostility that often prevailed over three decades. He has therefore followed his father in opening windows to his Central Asian neighbors. Ashgabat's regionalism has a solid economic rationale, and includes Taliban-ruled Afghanistan, which is the key to the transmission of Turkmen gas to Pakistan and India via the proposed TAPI pipeline.

Ashgabat's new regionalism extends beyond selling neighbors Turkmen gas and electricity. President Berdimuhamedov has begun visiting all the neighboring capitals. And he played an active part in the critically important meeting of the five Central Asian presidents, held at Issyk-Kul in Kyrgyzstan on 22 July of this year. At that meeting the presidents agreed that region-wide institutional structures were urgently needed to foster region-wide development and also to prevent outside powers from playing the countries off against each other in "divide and conquer" tactics. To be sure, Turkmenistan's UN-inscribed permanent neutrality will prevent it from joining certain projects relating to defense and security, but it is otherwise open to the creation of region-wide and exclusive consultative structures in dozens of fields.

This, then is the new regional basis on which Turkmenistan proposes to establish itself as a major player in the East-West and North-South transport of energy and other goods, including its own future manufactured products. Turkmenistan believes that cordial and productive relations with its Central Asian neighbors, including Afghanistan, will enable it to function more effectively in a world of major powers.

With respect to China Ashgabat has little room to maneuver, other than to balance its large gas sales to China with deliveries to the West. Significantly, the "West" in this case begins with Turkey. On 3 October Turkmenistan, hoping simultaneously to strengthen neighborhood relations and broaden its window to the West, joined the Organization of Turkic States initiated by NATO member Turkey. It had already purchased substantial numbers of Turkish-made Bayraktar TB2 UAV drone missiles and on 24 October, with recent events in Ukraine clearly in mind, proudly showed them off in a military readiness drill.

Turkmenistan's links with Russia remain, as always, close but complex. President Putin was well aware that Turkmenistan, while attending his Commonwealth of Independent States, did not participate in its security projects and that it had otherwise downgraded its participation in that organization. Viewing these developments in the context of Turkmenistan's balancing maneuvers with Turkey, and after a three-year standoff over pricing, Russia abruptly acceded to Ashgabat's rate and doubled its purchase of Turkmen gas. Sensing that he could no longer take for granted Turkmenistan's acquiescence with Kremlin policies, Putin, in a meeting with former president Gurbanguly Berdimuhamedov, expressed the hope that the new president would soon revert to a more compliant stance.

Turkmenistan's desire to overcome its physical isolation with new transport routes in every direction has caused it to redouble the export of gas to Iran and to significantly deepen its relations with the Gulf States. Persisting in its long-term goal of exporting gas to both Pakistan and India, Ashgabat has also reaffirmed its long-term links with Islamabad and, in April it received the President of India, Ram Nath Kovind, in a first time-ever visit. To the same end, it has received a *chargé d'affaires* from Taliban-ruled Afghanistan and treated him as a *de facto* ambassador. The Asian Development Bank remains committed to this ambitious project but, like other potential investors, has paused its involvement until Kabul gains some sort of diplomatic recognition.

Berdimuhamedov's Opening to Japan and the West

This, then is the regional and international context of Turkmenistan's recent demarches to Japan, the European Union, and the United States. Berdimuhamedov Sr. travelled to Tokyo to affirm and expand his country's existing links with Japan. After meetings with executives of a half dozen of Japan's top firms and after promising a more predictable environment for foreign investors, Ashgabat announced $11 billion worth of deals with Japan.

If Turkmenistan seeks balance's relations with all the major powers it must expand its links with both Europe and the United States. The best engine for doing so with Europe would be to export Turkmen gas there. Russia long blocked this, using the bogus argument that a trans-Caspian pipeline would pose an environmental danger to littoral states. The European Union, itself dependent on Russian gas, did not challenge Moscow's hegemonic stance on this issue. However, both Turkmenistan and Azerbaijan made a series of moves, albeit *sotto voce*, that can make greater trans-Caspian energy transport a reality. As a sign of the EU's rising interest, Charles Michel, president of its agenda setting body, the European Council, has proposed a joint conference on the reduction of methane emissions. This skirts the issue of bringing Caspian energy to Europe but it is a positive step, nonetheless. Methane emissions are a major problem of all former Soviet gas fields, including those in Turkmenistan, so the issue is real. However, the conference could also jump-start serious discussion on the export of Turkmen gas to Europe. This likelihood is all the stronger because Azerbaijan is deftly promoting the same cause, because Turkey foresees for itself a major future role in such activity, and because the EU itself has taken a leading role in mediating the generation-long conflict between Azerbaijan and Armenia over Karabakh.

If there now exists a path forward on the export of Turkmen gas, the road is still riddled with potholes. No sooner did Turkey step up as a key link in this trade than Vladimir Putin, on October 13, made the self-serving proposal that Russia could also export gas to Europe via the proposed Turkish hub. President Erdogan was quick to embrace the idea, but then fell silent in the face of EU embargos on the import of Russian energy.

These Turkmen-EU interactions, coming after a long period of negative interactions, set the context for several path-breaking new interactions between Turkmenistan and the United States. Turkmenistan has reminded Washington that after 9/11 it had opened its skies to American planes provisioning forces in Afghanistan and otherwise supported NATO logistics. Now it has welcomed the chance to revive Turkmenistan's partnership with the Montana National Guard that had existed for a decade and a half before President Obama terminated it in 2011. And early in October a group of major American executives and the U.S. ambassador to Ashgabat held a video conference with top Turkmen officials for a meeting of the Turkmenistan-U.S. Business Council. A visit to Turkmenistan by a team of American corporate CEO's is also being planned for December.

These changes were followed by a November 6-7 visit to Ashgabat by Donald Lu, Assistant Secretary of State and head of the Bureau of South and Central Asian Affairs. By starting his three-country tour in Turkmenistan, Lu signaled that Washington now considered it to be of the same level of importance as Uzbekistan and Kazakhstan. Reaffirming America's long-held commitment to Turkmenistan's "independence, sovereignty, and territorial integrity," Lu is reported also to have briefed the Turkmen on how they might beneficially deal with Washington's sanctions against Russia, noting how Kazakhstani investors had taken over local branches of several of the major Russian banks. Beyond this, Lu noted how the high world price of gas creates an unprecedented opportunity for Turkmenistan to send its gas westward via the much-discussed trans-Caspian pipeline. And, Lu added, Washington would support such a project.

Turkmen media also reported that Lu also suggested that the Turkmen economy will advance best by strengthening bilateral ties with the U.S and with the main international financial institutions. On its own, Ashgabat had already begun moving in this direction. It recently applied to join the World Trade Organization and received applicant status, but the path forward will place unprecedented demands on the Turkmen state. Realizing this and signaling that it is serious about addressing these demands, the Turkmen government for the first time sent a delegation of senior officials led by the vice-president to attend this year's annual joint conclave of the World Bank and International Monetary Fund.

The Regional Implications of Turkmenistan's Opening

Numerous developments in Turkmenistan suggest that that country has entered a fundamentally new phase of its development, with a strategy designed to overcome the isolation imposed by geography. Its new president, Serdar Berdymukhamedov, has prioritized transport and communications in all their dimensions as the key elements of that strategy. These present serious challenges for a people without a tradition of statehood, with little prior experience in governance, and a legacy of backwardness inherited from Soviet times. The fact that this country of only six million inhabitants also possesses the world's sixth largest reserves of natural gas presents grand opportunities, but equally formidable challenges as well. These include the need to strengthen its sovereignty and viability in a highly contested region, and to develop its physical and human resources in a manner that meets public expectations.

President Berdimuhamedov's formula for development is at once cautious and highly ambitious. As such, it gives rise to seeming anomalies. On the one hand he has preserved his predecessors' tradition of top-down control and carefully proscribed civic interactions with the outside world by blocking web sites and IP addresses deemed problematic. And, on the other hand, he has welcomed the renewal of the U.S.- sponsored Future Leaders Exchange Program (FLEX), that will enable numbers of Turkmen students to compete to study for a year in American high schools and live with American families. A positive step, to be sure, but one balanced by Ashgabat's announcement that a new Turkmen-Russian University will be launched in 2023.

Can Mr. Berdimuhamedov flesh out the details of his approach and sustain it amidst the inevitable setbacks that innovation always brings? That he succeeded his father helped assure that the transition of leadership was affected without strife, while the many initiatives noted above suggest a cautious but genuine openness to change.

Serdar Berdimuhamedov, who is seen as modest and self-disciplined, abjures public speaking. He studied agriculture in Turkmenistan and international affairs in Moscow and then served several years at Turkmenistan's embassy in Switzerland. He also brings a basic command of English and is computer literate, which mean that he can avail himself of global information sources.

While acknowledging the many constraints on change, it is clear that the world must reconsider old stereotypes and prepare to deal with a Turkmenistan that seeks to participate actively in the world economy and to benefit from doing so. This could bring a greater social openness in some areas, but the government will doubtless continue to calibrate this carefully in order to reinforce centripetal forces in society and maintain security. Overall, by engaging more actively with his Central Asian neighbors and with the global economy, and by introducing changes at home that will enable him to do so, Serdar Berdimuhamedov has challenged Turkmenistan's nearby and distant partners to revise and update their perception of his country and their policies towards it.

Conclusions

Turkmenistan has moved away from the isolationism that prevailed in Ashgabat since the United Nations endorsed it as a neutral country back in 1995. In its place, the country's new President has proposed what might be called "engaged neutrality." This new approach, announced in Berdymukhamedov's state of the union speech on September 23, finds expression in a focus on the transport of both energy and goods, in regional and continent-wide economic integration, and in macroeconomic reforms at home. This shift began under his predecessor, as was evident in 2021 in the abrupt end of the tensions with Azerbaijan over the contested *Dostluq* gas field in the Caspian, and Ashgabat's declared willingness to develop it together. But it has greatly accelerated under President Serdar Berdimuhamedov, and now shows every sign of continuing.

A principal challenge posed by this new direction will be to convince international financial institutions and investors in all sectors that the new course will find practical application in their projects and that it will endure through the years. As of now, the prospects appear positive. If they remain so, Turkmenistan may come to assume a pivotal regional role in energy cooperation and transport.

Uzbekistan 2.0: Continuity and Change in Foreign Policy

Farkhod Tolipov

Uzbekistan's foreign policy can roughly be divided into two periods, corresponding to its two Presidents, Islam Karimov and Shavkat Mirziyoyev. Despite Karimov's slogan "Turkistan is our common home," indicating an embrace of the wider region, territorial and water disputes in Central Asia overshadowed intra-regional affairs. Since Mirziyoyev came to power, Uzbekistan has taken dramatic steps to overcome such regional discord, instead emerging as a leader in building cooperation both on the region-wide level and through the budding alliance with Kazakhstan. Meanwhile, Tashkent's regional and international behavior has sometimes been quite cautious and hesitant, particularly as relates to great powers surrounding Central Asia. The question going forward, in particular against the background of Russia's war in Ukraine, is whether this approach verging on neutrality is sustainable, and whether Uzbekistan must emerge more assertively on the regional scene.

Uzbekistan's second President Shavkat Mirziyoev came to power in 2016 in a transition of power that was met with great expectations from the population. Many believe that this was the essential turning point in Tashkent's domestic and foreign policy since the country's independence. Yet there is both continuity and change in Uzbekistan's foreign policy that explain the country's international behavior. Some observers describe Uzbekistan's foreign policy as a pendulum movement, others as largely continuous. The dialectics of this process is determined by domestic factors such as the personalities of decision-makers as well as international factors related to the dynamics of the new world order.

Uzbekistan's Foreign Policy since Independence

Uzbekistan's foreign policy has evolved with the country's development throughout its period of independence, which can symbolically be divided into two stages: Uzbekistan 1.0 and Uzbekistan 2.0. The first stage is associated with the first President Islam Karimov and the so-called transition period.

Uzbekistan's first Foreign Policy Concept was adopted in 1993 and declared the following key principles of the country's foreign policy: non-participation in military-political blocks; active participation in international organizations; de-ideologization of foreign policy; non-interference in internal affairs of other states; supremacy of international law and priority of national interests. The second Foreign Policy Concept was adopted almost 20 years later.

In practice, however, Uzbekistan's foreign policy since the 1990s has been more sophisticated and controversial than doctrinally declared. Observers who have pointed to such controversies have described it as pendulum movement and the art of clever maneuvering on the international scene. This is a partially correct evaluation. From a more dialectical point of view, the international behavior of any state can be conceived as a fluctuation between engagement and disengagement since the international arena itself is full of controversial, troublesome, and uncertain situations. This is why retaining freedom of maneuver for different forms of engagements and disengagements in international affairs has been very characteristic of Tashkent's international stance from the very beginning.[1]

Foreign policy during the transition period was relatively efficient in terms of accomplishing international objectives pertaining specifically to this period. The most disturbing challenge to Uzbekistan's security stemmed from Afghanistan, where the civil war lasting from 1996 to 2001 subjected Tashkent to constant stress due to the risk of escalation and spillover. Karimov advanced a number of international initiatives from the UN platform to address the situation in Afghanistan, yet with mixed success.

Despite Karimov's slogan "Turkistan is our common home," indicating an embrace of the wider region, territorial and water disputes overshadowed intra-regional affairs, especially between Uzbekistan and Tajikistan over the construction of the Rogun hydropower station and between Uzbekistan and Kyrgyzstan over border delimitation and the construction of the Kambarata hydropower station.

Since independence Uzbekistan alongside other Central Asian states has experienced erstwhile unfamiliar geopolitical transformation. Tashkent faced and learnt geopolitics as it is.

---

1   Farkhod Tolipov, "Flexibility or Strategic Confusion? Foreign Policy of Uzbekistan", in *Uzbekistan Initiative*, Central Asia Program, the George Washington University, No. 2, February, 2014. (http://origin.library.constantcontact.com/download/get/file/1110347635144-152/UI+papers+2-Farkhad+Tolipov.pdf)

One of the dramatic implications of such a challenge was Russia's application for the membership in the then Central Asian Cooperation Organization (CACO) in 2004, which neither Tashkent nor Astana couldn't refuse. The outcome of such a distortion of composition of the Central Asian structure was that CACO was merged with the then Eurasian Economic Community (EvrAzES) in 2006. Since then, solely regional format of integration in Central Asia was frozen. This situation lasted almost a decade, until 2017.

At large, however, Tashkent managed to preserve a peaceful environment in the region. In one of its most important achievements during the first period, it managed to defuse the regional ambitions of particular states and firmly determine that it would not belong to someone else's sphere of influence. It also established new political and economic connections and sought self-affirmation as a member of the international community enjoying full rights, which would in the long run enhance its role in the region.[2] This new regional role was manifested with Mirziyoyev's ascent to power in December 2016 and the emergence of Uzbekistan 2.0.

Uzbekistan's New Course

From the very beginning of his term, Mirziyoyev proclaimed Central Asia to be the priority in Uzbekistan's foreign policy. This proclamation was a sign of Tashkent's new foreign policy course and constituted a revitalization of Karimov's proclamation that "Turkistan is our common home" from the early 1990s. Both continuity and innovation are visible in this approach. First, it should be noted that Mirziyoyev managed to unfreeze the regional

---

2   Resul Yalçın, *The Rebirth of Uzbekistan. Politics, Economy and Society in the Post-Soviet Era*, Reading: Ithaca Press, 2002, p.236.

format of interaction between the five Central Asian states by initiating a special mechanism, the Consultative Meetings (CMs) of presidents. This format proved to be relevant and functional; four meetings have already taken place within the framework, which is gradually evolving towards institutionalized regional integration.

Mirziyoyev managed to elevate relations with neighboring states to the highest level by signing special Strategic Partnership agreements and enhanced its cooperation with other important players in the region, including the U.S., Russia, China, Turkey, India, the EU, and Azerbaijan.

In December 2021, an unprecedented event took place in relations between Kazakhstan and Uzbekistan as the two states signed a Declaration on Alliance Relations. In November 2022 this document became a formal Treaty. The declaration envisaged the creation of a special institution, the Council of Heads of States, which could pave the way for a further institutionalization of the regional integration process.

Meanwhile, Mirziyoyev proclaimed a "New era of strategic partnership" during his visit to Washington in May 2018, where he confirmed Tashkent's commitment to the 2002 Declaration on Strategic Partnership between the U.S. and Uzbekistan. A new format for Strategic Partnership Dialogue was set up during the visit, accompanied with U.S. reaffirmation of its support for Uzbekistan's independence, sovereignty, and territorial integrity. Assistant Secretary of State Donald Lu welcomed Uzbekistan's ongoing program of reforms aimed at liberalizing the economy, promoting respect for human rights and protecting fundamental freedoms, and developing democratic institutions and civil society, and highlighted increasing U.S. assistance to support these reforms.³ A Strategic Partnership Dialogue took place in Washington in December 2022.

Until recently, Mirziyoyev's foreign policy has been conceived as pro-Russian. In 2021, Russia was Uzbekistan's number one foreign trade partner. However, the war in Ukraine became a serious challenge for Uzbekistan, which is directly affected by the implications of this war just like other former Soviet republics. On the one hand, Uzbekistan does maintain economic cooperation and business ties with Russia, despite the risk of being targeted by secondary sanctions. Thus, while Uzbekistan understands the tragedy of Ukraine, it does not want to sacrifice its cooperation with Russia. On the other hand, Tashkent cannot ignore the international community, particularly the West, which condemns Russia's aggression against Ukraine. The UNGA voting in April 2022 on Russia's aggression (where Uzbekistan did not vote) illustrates how delicate the situation is for countries like Uzbekistan.⁴

Another complicated issue of foreign policy priorities that has preoccupied Uzbekistan's policymakers for three years is the country's attitude towards the Eurasian Economic Union (EAEU). Political circles, the expert community, media and the public are divided as to whether Uzbekistan should become a member of this organization. Since December 2021, Uzbekistan has an observer status in EAEU, which is an ambiguous position that can last indefinitely.

At the same time, Tashkent's seemingly ambivalent policy hides a strong formulation and articulation of national interests.

---

3   "Joint Statement between the United States and Uzbekistan Following the Inaugural Meeting of the Strategic Partnership Dialogue," December 13, 2021. (https://uz.usembassy.gov/joint-statement-between-the-united-states-and-uzbekistan-following-the-inaugural-meeting-of-the-strategic-partnership-dialogue/)

4   Farkhod Tolipov, "Uzbekistan Between Ukraine and Russia: The Curse of Positioning," *Central Asia-Caucasus Analyst*, May 31, 2022. https://www.cacianalyst.org/publications/analytical-articles/item/13719-uzbekistan-between-ukraine-and-russia-the-curse-of-positioning.html.

According to Uzbekistan's former Minister of Foreign Affairs Abdulaziz Kamilov, "We are considering criticisms from the existing member countries ... We want to study their dissatisfaction,"[5] indicating that Tashkent takes into account the experiences of Kazakhstan and Kyrgyzstan from their EAEU memberships.

Foreign Policy Perceptions and Regional Geopolitics

For Uzbekistan, Central Asia has always been the highest foreign policy priority. Since independence, Uzbekistan has unequivocally taken the position that the five states of Central Asia represents a common and integrated region. In the early 1990s, Karimov proclaimed the concept "Turkestan is our common home" and advanced the slogan "Tajiks and Uzbeks are one people speaking two languages." This perception has persisted over more than 30 years of independence.

The process of regional integration has been complicated and affected by geopolitical deviations. In 2004, Karimov highlighted Central Asia's strategic uncertainty due to the intersecting interests of major powers in the region, forcing the regional states to navigate a complicated geopolitical landscape.

Although geopolitical and strategic uncertainty remains a key factor in regional politics, Mirziyoyev has announced that Central Asia will be (or remain) a priority in Uzbekistan's foreign policy. He managed to overcome misleading and counterproductive stereotypes about competition for regional leadership between Uzbekistan and Kazakhstan and make an example of the overall relationship between these two states for other neighbors.

---

5   Hashimova U. Uzbekistan still Contemplating Eurasian Economic Union Membership, https://thediplomat.com/2021/11/uzbekistan-still-contemplating-eurasian-economic-union-membership/ November 15, 2021.

Of special importance is the normative notion that Central Asian nations are fraternal peoples. Presidents and official representatives of the five regional states constantly make statements about their brotherly relationships, which have historically been shaped and nurtured. Some experts, however, question this thesis arguing that this normative aspect has limited relevance in regional affairs, which are dominated by realist views of national interests, pointing out numerous problems including border incidents that occur from time to time, various disputes over water management as well as narrow nationalist approaches to various other regional issues. However, the fact that these incidents have never escalated into critical international crises is often overlooked in the analysis of regional developments.

Without exaggeration, Uzbekistan (especially under the current president) has manifested itself as a positive example of friendly and fraternal attitudes towards neighbors. Practically, Uzbekistan's foreign policy in the region gives more impetus to micro-level integration alongside the macro-level processes mentioned above. Under Mirziyoyev, Uzbekistan has stimulated local level connectivity projects, creating and developing various forms of links (transport, business, cultural, sport) with provinces of neighboring countries.

There is great support in the region for these endeavors. Regional experts argue that the region has a special advantage – an ability to negotiate and to find compromise and mutually beneficial solutions, skills the countries concerned have demonstrated for many centuries.[6] Thus, Uzbekistan's efforts in the region are met with understanding, support and hope.

---

6   Rasul Rysmambetov, "Regional Fortress: Is Central Ala Ready to be Independent?" Turan Press, September 1, 2022. https://turanpress.kz/politika-i-vlast/3109-regionalnaja-krepost-gotova-li-centralnaja-azija-stat-samostojatelnoi.html

This was once again manifested during President Mirziyoev's state visit to Kyrgyzstan in February 2023. During that visit a big number of strategically important agreements were signed which symbolized significant breakthrough in their relations. Two states finally made it clear that all border issues were resolved. Also, the existing no visa regime was supplemented by the decision that citizens of both states can visit these two countries without putting stamps in their passport at the border-crossing points. Hopefully, this innovation will be an example for other neighboring states.

Meanwhile, Tashkent's regional and international behavior has sometimes been quite cautious and hesitant. For example, Uzbekistan demonstrated a neutral position during the UN voting against Russia for its aggression against Ukraine and later voted against Russia's exclusion from the UN Human Rights Council in April 2022. Uzbekistan's MFA stated that the Taliban is not a terrorist organization, although it is included in the international UN list of terrorist organizations. Uzbekistan maintains close ties with the Taliban, whereas Tajikistan rejects contacts with the organization and does not recognize its government. Uzbekistan does not dare to block Russian propaganda TV channels that dominate its information sphere, despite Tashkent's desire to demonstrate a neutral position towards Russia's war in Ukraine.

These and other controversies in Uzbekistan's foreign policy suggest that the country's foreign policy needs to be revised from a doctrinal point of view. Surprisingly, Uzbekistan's Foreign Policy Concept is a closed document, unavailable for public access.

Prioritized Issue Areas and Countries

The central and most complicated conceptual question of Uzbekistan's foreign policy is how to define the country's national interest in the world. The manner in which political parties, governmental bodies, and the media and expert communities formulate Uzbekistan's national interests is often influenced by lobby or oligarchic groups, the self-imposed "complex of a weak state," geopolitical biases, misinterpretations of history, and subjective preferences.

Thus, Uzbekistan's national interests should be accurately defined. The country's foreign policy is now in an awkward situation and in need of reform. From a fully realist perspective, Tashkent is preoccupied with national and regional security. The perception that the country and the whole region is located in a geopolitically turbulent area has stipulated very cautious and slow steps in foreign policy.

Uzbekistan does not prioritize any state in its foreign policy and has signed strategic partnership documents with geopolitical rivals such as the U.S. and Russia. As noted above, Uzbekistan's "moneybox of strategic partnerships" includes the U.S., Russia, China, the EU, Turkey, India, Pakistan, South Korea, Japan and all Central Asian neighbors. Yet Central Asia is set to remain the main priority in Tashkent's foreign policy, a fact underpinned by the practice of Consultative Meetings.

At the same time, Uzbekistan is objectively interested in developing strategic partnerships with leading actors in the international community, while its strategic partners are interested in such cooperation with Uzbekistan. In particular, the U.S. reportedly intends to deepen its ties with Uzbekistan, which will help Uzbekistan strengthen its security and reform process.[7]

Uzbekistan also intends to enhance its strategic partnership with the EU and was recently included in the EU's GSP+ system, signifying mutual support and interest in enhanced cooperation.

---

7   John C. Hulsman "America needs a strategic partnership with Uzbekistan," *The Hill,* September 9, 2022. https://thehill.com/opinion/international/3632514-america-needs-a-strategic-partnership-with-uzbekistan/

China is currently Uzbekistan's main foreign trade partner. Tashkent fully supports the ambitious "Belt and Road Initiative" which China proposed in 2013. The recent SCO summit in Samarkand once again demonstrated warm and friendly relations between the two states.

Strengths and Weaknesses of Uzbekistan's Foreign Policy

The self-imposed "complex of a weak state" not only limits Tashkent's freedom of maneuver on the international arena; it also creates moral and normative challenges for its domestic and foreign policies. Uzbekistan recently became a target of multiple information attacks and pressure from the Russian side. Any major attempt by the Uzbek government to articulate the importance of the state language (Uzbek), national values, independence and sovereignty, and positive relations with Western states habitually causes rapid and critical reactions from Russia.

Tashkent's foreign policy suffers from an excessive insistence of neutrality which, albeit not officially proclaimed like in the case of Turkmenistan, seems to be a *de facto* foreign policy principle. However, this is a special type of neutrality because it contrasts with Tashkent's eagerness to play a leading role in Central Asia and an active role on the international arena, especially when it comes to the situation in Afghanistan or its initiatives at the UN.

Uzbekistan's purported neutrality with regard to the war in Ukraine can also create the wrong impression, since both the political establishment and the expert community understand the reality and maintain a position that can be described as "tacit disagreement" with Russia.

Notably, Moscow frequently tests the strengths and weakness

of Uzbekistan's foreign policy through information attacks, to which Tashkent consistently responds with corresponding counter-messages.

However, this strategy has its limits; Russian propaganda still dominates Uzbekistan's information and media sphere, which cannot but affect public opinion and create ideologically and morally biased perceptions in society. A recent journalistic survey, for instance, revealed that a significant share of Uzbek citizens support Russia in its war with Ukraine.[8]

The Way Forward

First, increased dynamism of Central Asian regional integration is expected and urgent and Mirziyoyev should continue his leading role as an initiator and engine in this process.

Second, a vitally important issue in the near term is diversification of foreign economic relations and transport corridors. In particular, Uzbekistan has been articulating what is currently termed Central Asia-South Asia connectivity for years. Yet the implementation of this mega-project depends on peace and stability in Afghanistan, which will hardly be achieved in the near term. Another diversification option is through Caucasus (territories of Azerbaijan, Armenia and Georgia) which is acquiring real dynamism nowadays.

Third, it sems that Uzbekistan will in the coming years finally become a member of the World Trade Organization (WTO), which has been a long-term foreign policy objective. Some recent signs indicate real movement in this direction.

Fourth, Uzbekistan's leadership must overcome its (irrelevant,

---

8   "Rus propaganda mashinasi natizha beryapti. Özbekistondiklar kim tomonda?" [The Russian propaganda machine is paying off. Whose side are the Uzbeks on?], Rost Khabarlar, September 28, 2022. https://rost24.uz/uz/news/1179

or biased) neutrality as soon as possible, if it wants to forge an assertive, pro-active, efficient and independent foreign policy. The success of foreign policy is made up of four basic factors: adequate evaluation of the nation's power; a consistent formulation of national interests; a comprehensive foreign policy strategy (doctrine); and skilled diplomacy. These pillars of foreign policy must be strengthened and further developed.

Fifth, Tashkent should finally decide that the EAEU, which is a dubious, weak and irrelevant organization, has become even less attractive and workable in the context of the war in Ukraine and the sanctions regime imposed upon Russia, and give up any intention to become a member.

Analysts pointed out 20 years ago that "[T]he main challenge for Uzbekistan in its external relations is how to use these powers to advance its own interests without antagonizing others or succumbing to their hegemony."[9] One important question that can be added to this contemplation is what the country should do if the strategic partnership with a certain power objectively ceases to function in its full capacity and intent and even contradicts strategic partnerships with other powers.

---

9   Resul Yalçın, *The Rebirth of Uzbekistan. Politics, Economy and Society in the Post-Soviet Era*. (Ithaca Press, 2002), p.289.

Implications for Policy

Svante E. Cornell

The contributions to this volume have shown a complex and dynamic picture of the changing geopolitics of Central Asia and the Caucasus. What are the implications of these developments for the United States and Europe?

To begin with, let us answer the question why, ultimately, the changing geopolitics of this region matters to the West. It does in part because of the intrinsic value of these states: a group of open-minded, secular states in intersection of the Muslim world and Europe, who seek to become connected with the rest of the world and eschew dominance by one or two great powers. This makes them, by default, plausible long-term partners to the West. This in itself, warrants greater Western engagement with these countries.

Western engagement with these countries is also crucial because of the potential downside of geopolitical changes in the region. The war in Ukraine has accelerated the formation of an entente of sorts between Russia, China and Iran – an entente of revisionist and anti-Western powers. There is a plausible scenario in which these powers, or a combination of them, succeed in exerting dominance over the whole of Central Eurasia, creating an unbroken change of revisionist, autocratic domination ranging from the Sea of Japan to the Mediterranean and the eastern borders of the EU. Such a scenario would close off Central Asia and the Caucasus to Western access, thus limiting the West to the western periphery of the Eurasian continent. In turn, such a development would likely have profound implications for hesitant or recalcitrant Western partners like India and Turkey. Rather than continue to partner with the West, these powers would instead likely conclude that they ought to strike an arrangement of sorts with the revisionist entente powers.

Nothing in this analysis should be taken to ignore the very significant differences that exist among the powers of the revisionist entente, and with the hesitant Western partners, on the granular, local level. The signs of a Sino-Russian rivalry in Central Asia have been mentioned in this volume, as has the profound tensions between Iran and Turkey and between India and China. This entente exists largely as a result of an alignment at the global level, in opposition to American unipolarity and supposed Western hegemony, and could well fall apart in the medium term. But that does not change the fact that the stakes in Central Asia and the Caucasus are high not only for the local states but for Western interests at the regional and global level.

What, then, does this volume suggest Western powers do to avert such a scenario, and instead ensure that Central Asia and the Caucasus remain an area of geopolitical pluralism? Readers will doubtless draw their own conclusions from the study, but a few points are offered here as food for thought.

Focus on Security

A key conclusion from this study is that the central question in Central Asia and the Caucasus is that of security – at a basic level, that of the continued existence of sovereign states in Central Asia and the Caucasus. The Kremlin has indicated with full clarity that it no longer respects the independence, sovereignty, and territorial integrity of former Soviet states. More broadly, the behavior of regional and great powers in Eastern Europe, the Middle East, and East Asia suggests a sharp decline in the international norms that restrain regional and great powers from doing essentially what they think they can get away with in interfering in the internal affairs of smaller states. These are existential concerns that the states of the region are not well equipped to respond to.

This means that the issue of national security and defense has to occupy a much more central role in the approaches of the U.S. and EU to the region. While this will not come naturally to the EU, Brussels does have the ability to expand its assistance to the reform of the security sector in the region's states. As for the United States, it will find that regional states are cautious in discussions of security with Washington, fearing retribution from Beijing and Moscow. But this recalcitrance is in large part a function of the lack of trust in long-term American engagement in the region, a legacy of the decade in which the U.S. focused on announcing that it was intending to depart Afghanistan and the broader region, without much coordination with regional capitals.

Both the U.S. and European powers can support the upgrading of defense capabilities across the region, and cooperate with third parties that do so. And through NATO, both the U.S. and European powers can upgrade the Partnership for Peace's activities in the region. Key in this regard will be the Western role in Georgia, the country in which the West has had the largest security presence, but which is presently turning away from the West. Working to restore Georgia's Euro-Atlantic orientation should therefore take precedence in Western policy.

U.S.-EU Coordination

Related to the discussion on security above, it is clear that the U.S. and EU should work in a more coordinated way in the region. While a peace deal between Armenia and Azerbaijan has yet to be reached, U.S.-EU coordination on this process has advanced the peace process more than many observers expected. Similarly, when the EU and U.S. coordinated following the Russian invasion of Georgia, it succeeded in thwarting Russian objectives in that country to some degree, ensuring that the pro-Western government in Tbilisi survived. Going forward, consultations between the U.S. State Department and EU External Action Service on the region should expand, as should consultations between the NSC and the office of the EU Council President.

Involving Turkey

Turkey's newfound interest in Central Asia and the Caucasus is one of the major, and most positive developments in regional geopolitics in recent years. In the South Caucasus, Turkey emerged as a direct challenger to Russian dominance over the region in military and security terms. Its Defense Treaty with Azerbaijan signified a sea change in the power balance in the Caucasus, to the detriment of Iran and Russia. It is therefore in the interest of Western powers to explore coordination with Turkey in the region.

It is true that relations between the West and Turkey are

tense, and that Turkey's President Erdogan in many ways has por-
trayed himself as an opponent of Western supposed "hegemony."
This has enabled Erdogan to establish and maintain a positive
relationship with Vladimir Putin, even as Turkey has confronted
Russia in various specific contexts, be it Syria, Libya or the Caucasus. It is also true that Turkish suspicion of American intentions
is extremely high, primarily as a result of the U.S. decision to
prioritize backing of Syrian Kurdish forces that are loyal to the
PKK, an organization the U.S. itself recognizes as a terrorist group.

Precisely for this reason, however, the U.S. and the EU should
seek a dialogue with Turkey on Central Asia and the Caucasus.
Because this is an area where they have no substantial differences,
dialogue about this region could help rebuild rust between the
three sides on foreign and security policy matters more broadly.
Such dialogues should begin at the bureaucratic level within military, foreign policy and intelligence bureaucracies, and over time
advance to the political level. Because Turkey is already involved
in security matters in the region, Western partners should support
Turkey's involvement in beefing up the defense forces of Central
Asian states in particular.

Focusing on Middle Powers

Over the past decade, it has become clear that a gap is growing
in Central Asia and the Caucasus between countries that have
succeeded in establishing themselves as middle powers, and those
that continue to struggle to maintain their sovereignty. While
Azerbaijan, Kazakhstan and Uzbekistan belong to the former category, to one or another degree the smaller states all exhibit significant vulnerabilities. While the West should continue to focus
on providing development assistance to the smaller countries, the

implication is that on security and geopolitical issues they should focus on anchoring policies toward the region with the three middle powers, building long-term relationships of trust with the bureaucracies and societies of these three states. Over the long term, this will provide the West with the best possible conditions for maintaining a presence in Central Asia and the Caucasus and being able to positively influence developments there.

This will also mean altering Western rhetoric towards the region. In the past, Western powers have had a strongly normative approach to the region's states, very often treating them as less than equals and hectoring states on their records in human rights and democracy. The point here is not that the West should bury concerns over these issues. The point is that addressing those concerns in the way Western powers have done has not proven constructive, and hwas had as its main effect to alienate regional governments rather than obtaining results. Because the governments of the three middle powers have now embraced strategies of gradual reform, it makes sense for Western powers to adopt a more constructive approach to support these processes, and act as partners in reform initiatives. Western leaders will have to accept that in the short term this may not lead to the liberalization of political systems, but that the processes under way – if implemented – will provide the conditions for future democratic development. Because implementation of reforms is likely to be difficult and time-consuming, Western powers could play key roles in supporting these processes in cooperation with the pro-reform forces in regional governments.

Trans-Caspian Prospects

The Russian invasion of Ukraine and the Taliban takeover in Afghanistan have underlined the centrality of the Trans-Caspian connection for the economic development and, by extension, political independence of Central Asian states. While regional states have rapidly accelerated their diplomatic engagement on Trans-Caspian issues, the reality is that for the foreseeable future, the most likely result of their efforts will be the elimination of bottlenecks and the gradual expansion of transport corridors. But large infrastructural development, such as the building of new pipelines to connect Kazakhstan and Turkmenistan with Azerbaijan, is not likely to happen in the absence of large-scale external funding and political support.

Therefore, the U.S. and EU should systematically take stock of the needs in the region. They should also take cognizance of the private sector's reluctance to invest billions in infrastructural projects that could become redundant if Russian trade is suddenly opened up in the next few years. Therefore, Western powers should use their influence with International Financial Institutions and development banks to work for the provision of financing for large projects that could reduce the regional states' dependence on revisionist powers for their economic security. This means reducing Kazakhstan's dependence from Russia as well as Turkmenistan's dependence on China.

U.S. Bureaucracy Blues

As previously discussed in this volume, the U.S national security bureaucracy has shifted Central Asia back and forth between

Russia-centric and an Afghanistan-centric orbit, while maintaining the South Caucasus in the European orbit, where it is hardly a priority. It is time for the U.S. government to take a proactive approach to its bureaucratic map in order to prepare for the realities of the twenty-first century. Ideally, this would mean redrawing bureaucratic maps to create a bureau focused on the territory from Turkey's Aegean coastline in the West to Mongolia in the east, recognizing that small and mid-size states that seek to avoid dominance by regional powers are key to U.S. interests in Eurasia writ large. Such a redrawing of bureaucratic boundaries would acknowledge that this part of the world cannot be simply classified as either "Europe" or Asia," but constitutes an important world region in its own right. It would equip U.S. government officials with an ability to focus on this region and strengthen U.S. influence there, rather than the situation at present, where these parts of the world inevitably become an appendix to U.S. relations with often hostile powers.

If this proves too heavy a lift, the absolute minimum the U.S. government should do in the interim is to put an end to the practice where Central Asia is moved around in such a way that the National Security Council and State Department, as well as other agencies, put it in different parts of their bureaucracies, making any continuity of policy impossible.

Looking Ahead

As the preceding pages have shown, Central Asia and the Caucasus are undergoing a critical period, perhaps the most dangerous since their independence from the Soviet Union. Western powers played an important role in supporting the regional countries' transition to independence in the 1990s, and their efforts to connect to the world economy. But over time, Western efforts subsided, leaving these countries largely to their own devices. It is time for a rethink of U.S. and European approaches to the region. Happily, this does not primarily require the investment of large sums of money. What it primarily requires is a revision of the conceptual and bureaucratic approaches of Western powers toward this important region.

Contributors

Ariel Cohen, Ph.D., is a senior fellow at the International Tax and Investment Center (ITIC) where he heads the Energy, Growth, and Security Program (EGS). Dr. Cohen is the Founding Principal of International Market Analysis Ltd, and also a Non-Resident Senior Fellow with the Atlantic Council.

Svante E. Cornell is Director of the Central Asia-Caucasus Institute & Silk Road Studies Program, a Joint Center affiliated with the American Foreign Policy Council in Washington, D.C., and the Institute for Security and Development Policy in Stockholm.

Timur Dadabaev is Professor of International Relations and the Director of the Special Program for Japanese and Eurasian Studies at the Graduate School of Social Sciences and Humanities, University of Tsukuba, Japan.

Shairbek Dzhuraev is the co-founder and president of Crossroads Central Asia, and currently a Volkswagen Foundation postdoctoral research fellow at the OSCE Academy in Bishkek.

Kornely Kakachia is Professor of Political Science and Jean Monnet Chair at Ivane Javakhishvili Tbilisi State University, Georgia, and Director of the Tbilisi-based think tank Georgian Institute of Politics.

Halil Karaveli is a Senior Fellow with the Central Asia-Caucasus Institute & Silk Road Studies Program Joint Center, and Editor of the Turkey Analyst.

Nargis Kassenova is a Senior Fellow at the Program on Central Asia, Davis Center for Russian and Eurasian Studies, Harvard University.

Raffaello Pantucci is a Senior Fellow at the S. Rajaratnam School of International Studies (RSIS), and a Senior Associate Fellow at the Royal United Services Institute for Defence and Security Studies (RUSI). He is the author of the forthcoming Sinostan: China's Inadvertent Empire (Oxford University Press, April 2022.

Gulshan Sachdeva is Jean Monnet Chair and Coordinator Jean Monnet Centre of Excellence, School of International Studies at Jawaharlal Nehru University (JNU), New Delhi. He is also Book Series Editor, Europe-Asia Connectivity (Palgrave).

Brenda Shaffer is a research faculty member of the US Naval Postgraduate School. She also is a senior advisor for energy at the Foundation for Defense of Democracies think tank and a senior fellow at the Atlantic Council's Global Energy Center in Washington, DC.

S. Frederick Starr, Ph.D., is the founding Chairman of the Central Asia-Caucasus Institute, and a Distinguished Fellow with the American Foreign Policy Council.

Farkhod Tolipov is Director of the Non-Governmental Research Institution "Knowledge Caravan," Tashkent, Uzbekistan.

Anar Valiyev, Ph.D., is Associate Professor as ADA University in Baku, Azerbaijan.

Inara Yagubova is a Senior Research Fellow at the Institute for Development and Diplomacy in Baku, Azerbaijan.